Fisher Investments on Telecom

FISHER INVESTMENTS PRESS

Fisher Investments Press brings the research, analysis, and market intelligence of Fisher Investments' research team, headed by CEO and *New York Times* best-selling author Ken Fisher, to all investors. The Press covers a range of investing and market-related topics for a wide audience—from novices to enthusiasts to professionals.

Books by Ken Fisher
Debunkery
How to Smell a Rat
The Ten Roads to Riches
The Only Three Questions That Count
100 Minds That Made the Market
The Wall Street Waltz
Super Stocks

Fisher Investments Series
Own the World by
Aaron Anderson
20/20 Money by
Michael Hanson

Fisher Investments On Series
Fisher Investments on Energy
Fisher Investments on Materials
Fisher Investments on Consumer Staples
Fisher Investments on Industrials
Fisher Investments on Emerging Markets
Fisher Investments on Consumer Discretionary
Fisher Investments on Utilities
Fisher Investments on Health Care
Fisher Investments on Technology

FISHER
INVESTMENTS
PRESS

Fisher Investments on Telecom

Fisher Investments

with

Dan Sinton and
Andrew S. Teufel

WILEY

John Wiley & Sons, Inc.

Published by John Wiley & Sons, Inc., Hoboken, New Jersey.
Published simultaneously in Canada.

Important Disclaimers: This book reflects personal opinions, viewpoints and analyses of the authors and should not be regarded as a description of advisory services provided by Fisher Investments or performance returns of any Fisher Investments client. Fisher Investments manages its clients' accounts using a variety of investment techniques and strategies not necessarily discussed in this book. Nothing in this book constitutes investment advice or any recommendation with respect to a particular country, sector, industry, security; or portfolio of securities. All information is impersonal and not tailored to the circumstances or investment needs of any specific person.

Limit of Liability/Disclaimer of Warranty: While the publisher and author have used their best efforts in preparing this book, they make no representations or warranties with respect to the accuracy or completeness of the contents of this book and specifically disclaim any implied warranties of merchantability or fitness for a particular purpose. No warranty may be created or extended by sales representatives or written sales materials. The advice and strategies contained herein may not be suitable for your situation. You should consult with a professional where appropriate. Neither the publisher nor author shall be liable for any loss of profit or any other commercial damages, including but not limited to special, incidental, consequential, or other damages.

For general information on our other products and services or for technical support, please contact our Customer Care Department within the United States at (800) 762-2974, outside the United States at (317) 572-3993 or fax (317) 572-4002.

Wiley also publishes its books in a variety of electronic formats. Some content that appears in print may not be available in electronic books. For more information about Wiley products, visit our web site at www.wiley.com.

Library of Congress Cataloging-in-Publication Data:

Sinton, Dan.
    Fisher investments on telecom / with Dan Sinton and Andrew S. Teufel.
       p.   cm. — (Fisher investments press ; 20)
    Includes index.
    ISBN 978-0-470-52707-8 (hardback); ISBN 978-1-1180-6409-2 (ebk);
    ISBN 978-1-1180-6410-8 (ebk); ISBN 978-1-1180-6411-5 (ebk)
       1. Investments, Foreign. 2. International finance. 3. Investment analysis.
    4. Telecommunication—Economic aspects. I. Teufel, Andrew S. II. Title.
    HG4538.S4935   2011
    332.67'22—dc22
                                                              2010052435

Printed in the United States of America

10 9 8 7 6 5 4 3 2 1

Contents

Foreword

I'm pleased to introduce the tenth in a series of investing guides from Fisher Investments Press. This imprint—the first ever from a money manager—was launched in partnership with John Wiley & Sons to bring the accumulated investing wisdom of my firm to you, whether you're an investing enthusiast, student, or aspiring professional.

This isn't meant as a technical guide on the nuts and bolts of telephony. Rather, it's an investing guide. Like the other books in the *Fisher Investments On* series, it aims to help you make better, forward-looking forecasts on the sector, its industries, and its individual stocks. Each book in the series can stand alone—read one or just a few on topics that interest you. But together, they can be a comprehensive, do-it-yourself training program for capital markets analysis—done from the comfort of your couch. The series will eventually cover all the standard investing sectors (Energy, Materials, Consumer Staples, Health Care, Utilities, etc.—just Financials remains after this) as well as other investing regions and categories.

Telecom (official name: Telecommunication Services Sector) is currently about 5 percent of total world stocks (as measured by the MSCI All Country index). It's a small sector—globally, only Utilities is smaller. In the US, it's just 3 percent of the S&P 500—smaller than Utilities (as of 12/31/2010). But in capital markets, "small" never means "unimportant." Telecom firms don't manufacture the super cool, itty bitty but powerful computers we now call smartphones. Rather, they provide the service—fixed line, wireless, even some cable and satellite. Try making a phone call without that.

Besides the vital services Telecom firms sell, the sector can play an important role in a larger portfolio strategy. These firms are heavily regulated—because they provide a vital service. Demand for them doesn't stretch much in good times or snap back much in downturns. They are also very capital intensive—laying new fixed line and launching new wireless networks are very expensive. These features (and others described in the book) help make it a relatively less volatile sector and therefore classically defensive—it tends to do best in a bear market.

But not always! If you accurately forecast a bear market (never easy and difficult to repeat), you may not always want to overweight Telecom. There are traits to learn that sometimes make it fail. And always remember stocks look forward, not back, so it's seemingly perverse but perfectly normal for Telecom stocks to start outperforming just when sentiment seems particularly rosy and few foresee a bear market. This book describes what can help drive Telecom over- and underperformance in a variety of market environments—critical to building a well-diversified portfolio.

Regional analysis matters too. In developed nations, Telecom isn't (typically) seen as a growth industry. But in some Emerging Markets, penetration rates are still low and rising. Knowing if local regulation and trends favor fixed line versus wireless or some combination is key. Plus, unlike many other sectors, most Telecom firms typically don't sell services across country lines—though increasingly, progressive deregulation is starting to move the needle for international firms. Local regulation and politics can matter—a lot. The book shows you what to look for and gives you resources for staying on top of ever-changing global regulations.

What this book and others in the series won't do is give you hot stock tips or a set "formula" for finding them. In my third of a century-plus investing money for private clients and big institutions, I've never run across such a thing. Someone telling you otherwise is telling you more of what they don't know than what they do. Rather, this book provides a workable, repeatable framework for increasing the likelihood of finding profitable opportunities in the Telecom sector. And the good news is the investing methodology presented here works for all investing sectors and the broader market. This methodology should serve you not only this year or next, but the whole of your investing career. So good luck and enjoy the journey.

Ken Fisher
CEO of Fisher Investments
Forbes "Portfolio Strategy" Columnist
Four-time *New York Times* best-selling author

Preface

*T*he *Fisher Investments On* series is designed to provide individual investors, students, and aspiring investment professionals the tools necessary to understand and analyze investment opportunities, primarily for investing in global stocks.

Within the framework of a "top-down" investment method (more on that in Chapter 7), each guide is an easily accessible primer to economic sectors, regions, or other components of the global stock market. While this guide is specifically on Telecom, the basic investment methodology is applicable for analyzing any global sector, regardless of the current macroeconomic environment.

Why a top-down method? Vast evidence shows high-level, or "macro," investment decisions are ultimately more important portfolio performance drivers than individual stocks. In other words, before picking stocks, investors can benefit greatly by first deciding if stocks are the best investment relative to other assets (like bonds or cash), and then choosing categories of stocks most likely to perform best on a forward-looking basis.

For example, a Telecom sector stock picker in the late 1990s probably saw his picks soar as investors cheered the so-called New Economy. However, from 2000 to 2002, he probably lost his shirt. Was he just smarter in the late 1990s than he was in 2000? Unlikely. What mattered most was stocks in general, and especially Technology and Telecom stocks, did great in the late 1990s and poorly entering the new century. In other words, a top-down perspective on the broader economy was key to navigating markets—stock picking just wasn't as important.

Fisher Investments on Telecom will guide you in making top-down investment decisions specifically for the Telecom sector. It shows how to determine better times to invest in Telecom, what Telecom industries are likelier to do best, and how individual stocks can benefit in various environments. The global Telecom sector is complex, covering different industries and countries with unique characteristics. Using our framework, you can be better equipped to identify their differences, spot opportunities, and avoid major pitfalls.

This book takes a global approach to Telecom investing. Most US investors typically invest the majority of their assets in domestic securities; they forget America is less than half of the world stock market by weight—over 50 percent of investment opportunities are outside our borders, and even more when you include emerging markets. While a relatively large proportion of the world's Telecom weight is based in the US, there remain many investment opportunities overseas. Given the vast market landscape and diverse geographic operations, it's vital to have a global perspective when investing in Telecom today.

USING YOUR TELECOM GUIDE

This guide is designed in three parts. Part I, "Getting Started in Telecom," discusses vital sector characteristics and the history of the sector since Alexander Graham Bell invented the first practical telephone.

Part II, "Next Steps: Telecom Details," provides an overview of the sector's two industries and walks through the next step of sector analysis. We discuss the most important economic, political, and sentiment factors that drive Telecom's relative performance. We also explore some of the most influential consumer trends driving demand for Telecom services and products and the resulting challenges and opportunities.

Part III, "Thinking Like a Portfolio Manager," delves into a top-down investment methodology and individual security analysis. You'll learn to ask important questions like: What are the most important elements to consider when analyzing wireline and wireless service providers? What are the greatest risks and red flags? This book gives you a five-step process to help differentiate firms so you can identify ones with a greater probability of outperforming. We also discuss a few investment strategies to help determine when and how to overweight specific industries within the sector.

Fisher Investments on Telecom won't give you a silver bullet for picking the right Telecom stocks. The fact is the "right" Telecom stocks will be different in different times and situations. Instead, this guide provides a framework for understanding the sector and its industries so that you can be dynamic and find information the market hasn't yet priced in. There won't be any stock recommendations, target prices, or even a suggestion of whether now is a good time to be invested in the Telecom sector. The goal is to provide you with tools to make these decisions for yourself—now and in the future. Ultimately, our aim is to give you the framework for repeated, successful investing. Enjoy.

Acknowledgments

This book is a collaboration of many people that deserve thanks and praise. We would like to thank Ken Fisher for providing the opportunity to write this book and Jeff Silk for his encouragement—without them, the concept and execution of the book would be impossible. Our colleagues at Fisher Investments also deserve thanks for continually sharing their wealth of knowledge, insights, and analysis. Special thanks to Jessica Wolfe, Matt Schrader, Brian Kepp, Mike Hanson, Saied Ezzeddine, Evelyn Chea, and Leila Amiri.

We owe innumerable thanks to Lara Hoffmans for her assistance and considerable editing contributions. Her encouragement and wit guided the book from inception to print.

Marc Haberman, Molly Lienesch, and Fabrizio Ornani were also instrumental in the creation of Fisher Investments Press, which created the infrastructure behind this book. Of course this book would also not be possible without our data vendors, so we owe a big "thank you" to Thomson Reuters, Global Financial Data, and Standard & Poor's. We'd also like to thank our team at John Wiley & Sons, for their support and guidance throughout this project, especially Laura Walsh and Kelly O'Connor.

Dan Sinton would also like to express gratitude to Sabrina "Pookie" Soulis for her unwavering encouragement through the book-writing process.

GETTING STARTED
IN TELECOM

I

TELECOM BASICS

How we communicate today is largely a direct result of the transformation of the Telecommunication Services (i.e., "Telecom") industry. Drums, smoke signals, semaphores, and carrier pigeons are out. Mobile phones, e-mails, and tweets are in. Today, even remote campsites have wireless Internet connections. In developing countries, many people without electricity and running water in their homes still have cell phones! This dramatic increase in access to information has changed the way we live, to say the least. Thanks to modern telecommunications, we now know what is going on globally in real time. So much information can be overwhelming, however, especially when it comes to investing in the stock market. What is noise and what is actually important?

The purpose of this guide is to create a structure and process for investing in the Telecom sector. Also, note this is an *investment* guide to Telecom, not a *technical* guide. We're not going to scrutinize the differences between CDMA2000 and CDMA2000 1xEV-DO. Instead, you will learn what questions to ask and the critical thinking required to understand what makes Telecom likely to perform better

A Little Bird Told Me

People have always sought timely and superior telecommunications to prosper. In 1815, the British surprised the world by defeating Napoleon's army at Waterloo. The news spread slowly from the battlefield, but in London, Nathan Rothschild learned the outcome before anyone else. How? By employing cutting-edge telecommunication—carrier pigeons. When he received the news, Mr. Rothschild bought British government debt securities (which subsequently shot up when the public learned the result of the battle) and added to his family's legendary fortunes.

or worse than the overall market in the period ahead—over the next 12, 18, or 24 months at the outset. By learning the process for forming a forward-looking opinion, you'll also learn to pick what types of Telecom stocks are likely to be best for the prevailing economic conditions, political environment, and market sentiment.

TELECOM 101

These days, the term *telecommunication* often refers to an electronic transmission of signals via telephony, radio, television, etc., but for our purposes, it primarily applies to telephony companies (more on why in the Sector Composition chapter). Telecom firms traditionally sold just landline phone services, but have now expanded their offerings to wireless phones, Internet access, and even television. Providing such services requires tremendous capital investments—just think of the incredible web of phone lines and cell phone towers connecting the whole world. Because of the high costs involved, Telecom firms have historically been either government owned or monopolies and are therefore heavily regulated. However, with time comes change—the speedy pace of innovation and new technologies has driven progressive deregulation in the Telecom sector. Ma Bell (a term referring to the Bell System organization, formerly led by the American Bell Telephone Company and AT&T) is no longer the only player in town, and many firms now compete to provide customers a variety of services.

Thank the French

For millennia, humans have communicated over distances, but it wasn't until the 1930s that the French coined the word télécommunication, from *télé-* "at a distance" + *communication*, obviously, "communication." Although the French typically refuse to tarnish their language with foreign words, the world demonstrated greater tolerance and added the word to its lexicon.

Despite such change and greater diversity in the types of Telecom companies, they all share general characteristics. Typically, firms in the Telecom sector:

- Have defensive characteristics
- Provide services with relatively inelastic demand
- Are capital intensive
- Are heavily regulated

A DEFENSIVE SECTOR

When the broader market rallies, the Telecom sector has traditionally underperformed, but when the broader market falls, Telecom often remains relatively resilient—this is the sector's defining characteristic. And as a typically *defensive* sector, Telecom:

- Typically performs better than the market during bear markets
- Has lower volatility relative to the market
- Usually pays a dividend

Best in a Bear

One could say that in any given year, the stock market can do only one of four things: It can go up a lot, up a little, down a little, or down a lot—a bear market. During a bear market, most sectors, if not all, will fall—even those generally considered defensive (such as Telecom, Health Care, Consumer Staples, and Utilities, for example). Though a defensive sector, like Telecom, may be down on an absolute

Table 1.1 S&P 500 Telecom Versus S&P 500 Composite in Bear Markets

Bear Market Start	Bear Market End	S&P 500 Telecom	S&P 500 Composite	Relative Return
12/31/1961	**06/30/1962**	**–24.9%**	**–22.2%**	**–2.7%**
01/31/1966	09/30/1966	–11.2%	–15.7%	4.5%
11/30/1968	06/30/1970	–25.9%	–29.2%	3.3%
12/31/1972	09/30/1974	–16.2%	–42.7%	26.5%
11/28/1980	08/12/1982	28.4%	–16.7%	45.1%
08/31/1987	11/30/1987	–11.2%	–29.6%	18.4%
07/16/1990	10/11/1990	–7.6%	–19.2%	11.6%
03/24/2000	**10/09/2002**	**–73.9%**	**–44.8%**	**–29.1%**
10/09/2007	03/09/2009	–47.6%	–55.3%	7.6%
Annualized Bear Market Returns		**–23.3%**	**–27.8%**	**4.6%**

Source: Global Financial Data, Inc., S&P 500 Index Total Returns, S&P 500 Telecom Index Total Returns. Closest month-end price from 12/26/56 to 8/30/89; daily data from 9/11/89 to 3/9/09.

basis, it's also more likely to outperform the market on a relative basis. As an example, the broad market might fall 30 percent in a bear market, but a defensive sector might be down 10 percent—which is a positive 20 percent relative spread.

Table 1.1 shows annualized returns for the S&P 500 and the S&P 500 Telecom Sector during the last nine bear markets. (Though we generally encourage you to think globally, we are using US stock data here because we have more historical sector-specific data. Also, because the US stock market is large and well diversified, it can at times serve as a useful proxy for global stocks.) Telecom has underperformed the broad market only twice during a bear market—in 1962 and the 2000–2002 bear market. Most times, Telecom outperformed during a bear.

However, Telecom's limited sensitivity to a booming economy means Telecom has underperformed in six out of the eight last bull markets (shown in Table 1.2). Again, note that in a bull market, Telecom can rise too, but probably not as much as the broad market. Here, we are focusing on the performance relative to the broad

Table 1.2 S&P 500 Telecom Versus S&P 500 Composite in Bull Markets

Bull Market Start	Bull Market End	S&P 500 Telecom	S&P 500 Composite	Relative Return
06/30/1962	01/31/1966	37.1%	89.6%	−52.4%
09/30/1966	11/30/1968	21.9%	51.6%	−29.7%
06/30/1970	12/31/1972	51.3%	75.6%	−24.3%
09/30/1974	11/30/1980	87.3%	195.2%	−107.8%
07/31/1982	**08/31/1987**	**288.2%**	**278.3%**	**9.9%**
11/30/1987	07/16/1990	57.8%	75.7%	−17.9%
10/11/1990	03/24/2000	447.6%	546.2%	−98.6%
10/09/2002	**10/09/2007**	**171.1%**	**110.4%**	**60.7%**
Annualized Bull Market Return:		**18.0%**	**21.7%**	**−3.7%**

Source: Global Financial Data, Inc., S&P 500 Index Total Returns, S&P 500 Telecom Index Total Returns. Closest month-end price from 12/26/56 to 8/30/89; daily data from 9/11/89 to 3/9/09.

market. And there have been notable periods when Telecom has significantly outperformed, even during a bull market. Understanding the Telecom sector can help investors identify those periods and determine how to optimally position their portfolios.

Bear Market Telecom Bets

Telecom has fairly consistently outperformed during bear markets and underperformed during bull markets. Consider this: Absent taxes and trading costs, if you'd invested $1 million in the S&P 500 Composite in 1962, you'd have earned approximately $72 million by the end of 2009.[1] However, if you'd played defense by putting your entire portfolio in the Telecom sector during every bear market, you'd have approximately $122 million. That's a whopping $50 million more![2]

Sounds great! Except such a move is likely foolhardy for most investors. It's extraordinarily difficult to call the top and the bottom of a bear market precisely and even more difficult to do so with any degree of consistency. Plus, putting your entire portfolio in one sector is a massive bet that, should you be wrong, could seriously harm your relative performance for years to come. (For more information on forecasting bear markets, see Ken Fisher's *The Only Three Questions That Count*.)

Because bull markets tend to be longer and stronger than bear markets, the Telecom sector has often lagged the market for considerable periods of time. But its value as a defensive sector is reason enough to not ignore Telecom.

Low Volatility

Another characteristic contributing to Telecom's defensive nature is the sector's historically lower volatility relative to the market.

Why is understanding volatility so important? When investing, it is paramount to understand not only potential returns or rewards, but risks too. If we take more risk, we expect to earn a higher rate of return. But how best to assess risk? Although the best method for computing risk is fiercely debated, the most common method and the one we will use is an investment's historical volatility, or *beta*. Beta describes a given stock's (or sector's) historical returns in relation to the returns of the stock market as a whole. A beta of less than one means the stock tends to be less volatile than the market, whereas a beta of more than one indicates the stock tends to be more volatile than the market.

Figure 1.1 shows the beta of the MSCI World Telecom Sector in relation to the MSCI World Index over rolling five-year periods. Over the last 35 years, Telecom's average beta has been 0.71—one of the lowest-beta sectors, along with other traditionally defensive sectors like Utilities, Health Care, and Consumer Staples. Theoretically, this means if the MSCI World Index moves up (or down) 10 percent, the Telecom sector tends to move up (or down) 7.1 percent.

Figure 1.1 shows Telecom has historically been much less volatile than the market, with the exception of the dot-com and telecom madness in the late 1990s that ended dramatically in 2000. Even more striking is Telecom's upward sloping trend line, which has been increasing since the early 1980s. (Bookmark this page. By the time you've finished reading this guide, you should be able to apply your knowledge of things like high inflation in the late 1970s and regulatory trends to hypothesize what caused major moves on this chart. By understanding the past, we can hope to be more proficient at forecasting the future.)

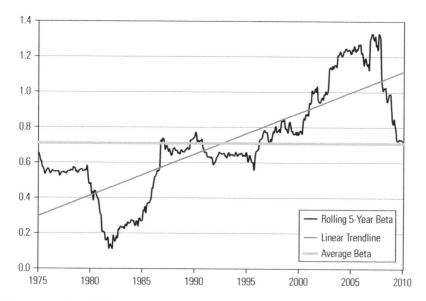

Figure 1.1   Telecom Sector Beta Relative to MSCI World Index (12/31/74–12/31/09)

Source: MSCI Original Classification Sector Index from 12/31/1969 to 12/30/1994, MSCI, Inc.,[3] MSCI World Index from 12/31/69 to 12/31/09. Beta calculated using rolling five-year monthly total returns.

Although Telecom again proved its defensive nature in the recession of 2007 to 2009 when its beta fell back to its historical average, the progressive deregulation over the last couple decades has likely increased competition within the sector, as well as overall volatility. Moreover, Telecom services like mobile phones, Internet access, and television may be more discretionary in nature than the traditional landline, contributing to more volatility in companies' performance.

Low volatility helps the sector outperform during a bear market, but it has uses in all market conditions as well. Blending components that move differently—i.e., have different degrees of volatility—is a standard diversification tactic. And diversification in any market condition is a smart risk management strategy.

High Dividend Yields

Telecom firms also tend to have fairly high, stable dividends, which is another common characteristic of classically defensive sectors. As

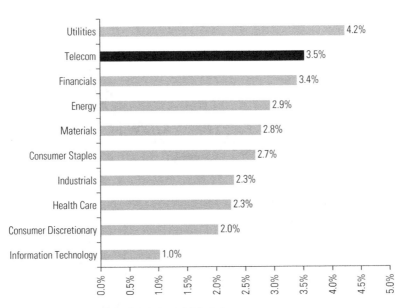

Figure 1.2   Sector Dividend Yields

Source: Thomson Reuters, MSCI Inc.,[4] annualized yield from 12/31/99 to 12/31/09.

Figure 1.2 illustrates, over the last decade, Telecom has provided a higher dividend yield than every sector other than Utilities.

A dividend represents a return of profit to shareholders. Some firms pay dividends, others don't, preferring to reinvest profits into firm growth—neither necessarily results in better or worse total return over time. Because Telecom companies have relatively steady cash flows and historically limited growth opportunities, they tend to distribute profits through dividends rather than reinvesting profits. Many investors like the perceived safety of higher dividends, which helps contribute to greater demand for Telecom during economic downturns and bear markets.

But keep in mind: While many investors consider dividends to be safe, this is perception only. (Though in the near term, perception—i.e., sentiment—can be a powerful demand driver.) Dividends are not a guaranteed source of income. Dividends are only as good as a company's fundamental business prospects because a company can't pay a dividend if it is unable to generate sufficient capital to do so. (Many investors will

Dividends and Taxes

One of the most important factors in determining the value of dividends is tax policy. Although different investors have different tax considerations, dividends may be taxed at a different rate than normal income or long-term capital gains. When tax rates change, it could materially affect the value of dividends relative to other forms of income. Further, tax policy can influence whether a firm chooses to pay a dividend and how much.

remember well when numerous firms slashed their dividends or stopped them entirely during 2008.) Moreover, while an 8 percent dividend yield may sound attractive, a higher dividend yield is often reflective of a riskier stock—or a perception that the dividend might be cut.

Instead of focusing on dividend yield, investors should care about *total return*—price appreciation plus dividends accrued. But specifically during market downturns, a sector's dividend yield can influence investor demand.

INELASTIC DEMAND

Telecom has tended to be a low-risk, low-reward sector. But what is it about Telecom that makes its shares so resilient during a downturn, less volatile than the market, and allows its firms to pay stable dividends? Generally, the key to stable share prices is stable cash flow and earnings. From year to year, Telecom firms are able to generate relatively consistent—albeit relatively low—earnings growth. This is largely due to relatively inelastic demand, capital intensity, and regulation of the Telecom industry.

Basic utilities like water, electricity, and gas are difficult for consumers to give up. Phone services aren't far behind. Even when they become less affordable (e.g., prices rise or incomes fall), it's difficult to adjust consumption without having a significant negative impact on daily life. For example, even if you lose your job, you're likely going to keep your phone service—you need to be able to answer the phone when that next job comes calling. In economic terms, this makes demand for basic telecom services *inelastic*.

This has three important implications. First, it means demand for telecom services isn't as economically sensitive to income growth or economic activity as more discretionary sectors (like Consumer Discretionary, Energy, or Materials). In fact, over the past two decades, the percentage of household spending committed to communication services versus other budgetary items has increased. Despite the increase, communication services still accounts for only 2.2 percent of household budgets in the US—a level still relatively affordable.[5] Although an economic downturn would reduce the number of businesses and employees who need phones, demand is usually much less impacted than it would be for durable goods like new cars or washing machines. This is another important factor that improves Telecom's relative resilience during an economic downturn.

Second, it means that Telecom firms, if unchecked by regulation and competition, could significantly raise prices without reducing consumption much.

Third, the essential, irreplaceable nature of telecommunications means the government has a big interest in ensuring the population gets reliable, cost-effective service from Telecom firms. Without telecom services, businesses can't function, people can be economically and socially unhappy, and politicians will likely lose their jobs. And because politicians really don't like losing their jobs, the government often takes an active role in regulating the sector (though this doesn't necessarily have the intended effects of improving reliability and reducing costs for consumers).

A CAPITAL INTENSIVE SECTOR

Capital intensity refers to how much fixed capital investment is required in the production process—and few businesses require more fixed capital investment than Telecom firms. A tremendous amount of upfront investment in equipment and infrastructure is required before a Telecom firm can provide services and start generating revenue.

Moreover, in order to offset declining per-minute calling prices and increase company sales, Telecom firms must spend to adapt to rapidly changing market conditions and new service offerings. Fixed line providers need to increase fiber-optic infrastructure, and wireless companies are continually upgrading to offer higher speed data services. In 2007, Organisation of Economic Co-operation and Development (OECD) telecommunications investment reached $185 billion![6]

Figure 1.3 shows fixed asset investment relative to annual revenue—in other words, how much in fixed asset investment is required to drive a dollar of revenue. Telecom is currently second among the standard sectors—requiring about $2 in fixed asset investment for every $1 in annual revenue.

Capital Market Dependence

Because telecoms are required to make large capital outlays, which can take years to generate any revenue, they are highly dependent on

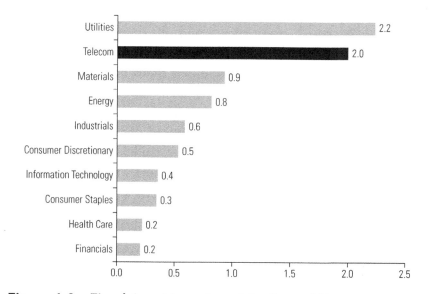

Figure 1.3   Fixed Asset Investment to Annual Revenue

Source: Standard & Poor's Research Insight®,[7] 12/31/09. Fixed Assets calculated as Property, Plant & Equipment plus Accumulated Depreciation.

investors to provide long-term financing. There are basically two ways to do this: issuing stock or issuing bonds.

Since Telecom firms usually trade at low earnings multiples (low P/E ratios), so issuing stock is often unattractive—it may not be worth diluting earnings if you receive a low valuation for each share you sell. Issuing debt is often more enticing—Telecom companies tend to have much more stable, predictable earnings than most companies, there is less risk of default, and they can therefore borrow at lower interest rates. Furthermore, issuing bonds has a benefit: Interest payments are tax-deductible, which can help offset the taxes paid on profits returned to shareholders via dividends. However, as a company issues more debt, the risk the company won't be able to make its interest payments increases. If a firm issues too much debt, its credit rating may be downgraded by ratings agencies, and it could become more challenging for the company to obtain financing. Nevertheless, due to their stable businesses, Telecom companies are usually able to have significantly more leverage than most sectors.

Economies of Scale

Heavy infrastructural requirements and their considerable financing expenses lead to high fixed costs for the industry. In other words, whether AT&T is servicing one client or a thousand, a lot of its costs (e.g., its interest expense) will stay the same. This creates tremendous *economies of scale*, meaning telecoms can significantly reduce their average per-unit costs by increasing customers and distributing their fixed costs across a greater number of subscribers. Said another way, assuming the same level of service, each new subscriber will be more profitable than the last. If telecoms aren't maximizing their *capacity utilization*, they aren't providing their services at the lowest possible cost or maximizing their profit potential.

REGULATION

For most of its modern existence, the Telecom sector has been the subject of heavy government regulation. In fact for much of the twentieth century, many of the world's largest Telecom companies were owned by governments outright. Even today's publicly traded telecoms tend to have high government ownership, which begs the question: Why does the government play such an active role in the Telecom sector?

Regulatory intervention has been necessary to transform monopolistic telecommunication markets into competitive ones. The high capital intensity of Telecom has acted as a barrier to entry for competition. In order to ensure monopolies do not abuse their dominant position, extensive regulation has been required to ensure the sector functions as reliably and cost-effectively as possible. Also, as previously mentioned, regulation reflects the essential and irreplaceable nature of telecommunications. Without communications, economies—and likely the incumbent governments—would collapse, providing governments with a very strong incentive to regulate the industry.

Today, most Americans can afford a mobile phone, which costs practically nothing compared to the first cell phone (which cost $3,995 when it debuted in 1983—and was the size of a shoebox. Over time, new technologies have made traditional services cheaper and new services available at reasonable costs. In this way, technology has helped deliver the market conditions regulators have sought and has therefore made possible a policy of progressive deregulation in the Telecom sector.

In general, progressive deregulation has increased competition and expedited the commoditization of telecom services. The result has been customers in both fixed and mobile telephony have greater bargaining power, which led to better services and prices and diminished the need for heavy government regulation. Over the past couple decades, the Telecom sector has increasingly begun to resemble other industries, in which companies are able to compete not only domestically, but internationally.

The Goal of Telecom Regulators

The objectives of regulators differ from one country to another. But in general, they all view telecommunications as an essential public service and therefore seek a regulatory environment conducive to a

Investing Without Emotion

The role the government should play in the economy is perhaps one of the most hotly contested issues of all time—and the Telecom sector has often been at the center of the debate. However, investors are usually best served by focusing not on how they think the sector *should* be regulated, but on how it actually is regulated and the likely impact on investment performance.

myriad supply of services. Some of the widely accepted regulatory objectives are to:

- Promote universal access to basic telecommunication services
- Foster competitive markets to promote efficient supply of services, quality, advanced services, and efficient prices
- Prevent abuses of market power
- Create a favorable climate to promote investment to expand networks
- Promote public confidence
- Protect consumer rights[8]

Regulation, Risk, and Reward

Usually, the more vigorously regulated a Telecommunications company, the less opportunity it has to earn outsized profits and generate large returns for shareholders. However, a highly regulated company often faces no competitive pressure or price fluctuations for its products and can usually count on fairly stable earnings, limiting the risk for investors.

There are pros and cons of regulation—for both consumers and investors. By limiting the risk for investors, regulation theoretically lowers the cost of capital for Telecom companies, allowing the savings to be passed on to consumers. But if a telecom is highly regulated and almost guarantees a return on its investments, it has little incentive to operate efficiently and may make investments that are entirely unnecessary. This can significantly raise costs for consumers.

Understanding the manner and degree to which Telecom is regulated is critical to investors. In Chapter 4, we delve into Telecom regulation in more depth.

Public Policy Shifts

It's often changes in regulations that have the biggest impact on the Telecom sector and company share prices. As political sentiment shifts from the right to the left and back, public policies can also shift dramatically.

When the government decides to change the rules, it usually creates winners and losers, making it important for Telecom investors to be acutely aware of the political environment. But it is difficult to determine if, when, and how public policy will change—and equally difficult to figure out exactly how it will affect the sector: Which companies will be winners and which companies will be losers?

Due to the progressive nature of deregulation in Telecom and the uncertainty it creates, the sector's composition and drivers will be examined in detail to increase our chances of identifying which investments may be best positioned for the future.

Chapter Recap

You've now been introduced to some of the fundamental characteristics of the Telecom sector. In later chapters, we build upon many of the concepts presented here, including the following:

- The Telecom sector is highly defensive and tends to perform best on a relative basis during bear markets.

- Telecom has generally been a low-growth, low-return sector due to the maturity of the industry and regulation. As a result, Telecom tends to return a large portion of its income to shareholders via dividends.

- Due to high capital costs and network infrastructure requirements, elevated debt and barriers to entry have almost always existed.

- Because telecoms have often been state-owned or monopolies and provide essential services, government regulation has been heavy.

- Technology has helped drive deregulation, which can have a major impact on the sector.

2

A BRIEF HISTORY OF THE TELECOM INDUSTRY

In 1915, the first transcontinental phone call was made from New York to San Francisco. Now, the globe is interconnected via various traditional, wireless, and Internet-based technologies. Innovation has been constant—sometimes faster, sometimes slower. And by understanding the past and how we arrived at the present, investors can have a better idea of where Telecom may be going.

This chapter briefly documents the early development of the Telecommunications sector in the United States and the regulation that transformed it.

THE EARLY YEARS

The history of telecommunications is ancient. And while we could begin with smoke signals, they didn't present much of an investment opportunity. For our purposes, we'll start with the telephone—the birth of the Telecom sector as we know it.

Alexander Graham Bell—Father of the Modern Telephone

Alexander Graham Bell is recognized with inventing the first practical telephone. (Less well known is that he had a deaf mother and wife and was a third-generation elocutionist who taught Helen Keller.) But it was a race to the finish line. Elisha Gray (an assistant to Thomas Edison) and Bell filed similar patents on the same day in 1876. Bell ultimately received the patent, though he was accused of stealing the telephone from Gray, and numerous lawsuits ensued. The accusations still fly to this day, but no matter—Bell subsequently created the Bell Telephone Company in 1877, which evolved into the American Telephone & Telegraph Company (AT&T) in 1885.

Initially, people were so familiar with and enamored by the telegraph, few realized the incredible impact the phone would have on global business and society. In fact, Western Union passed on buying Bell's patents for a measly $100,000 (approximately $5 million in 2010 dollars)[1] because it considered the phone a passing novelty.[2] Even so, telephones didn't pose a real risk for Western Union and the telegraph for about 20 years.

It wasn't until 1893 that the Bell patents expired, which resulted in greater competition that was beneficial to consumers but bad for AT&T. During its 17 years of patent protection (1876–1893), AT&T was able to earn a 46 percent return on investments.[3] But the patent expiration led to increased competition, and by 1906, the company was earning only 8 percent on investments.[4]

The story for consumers was the opposite. In 1893, there were only 270,000[5] phones in the US and the average number of daily calls per 1,000 Americans was 37.[6] However, in 1900—seven years after the Bell patents expired—the number of phones jumped to six million,[7] and the average number of daily calls skyrocketed to 391 per 1,000 Americans.[8]

Despite the clear benefits of competition for consumers—more phones and more calls—the US government eventually passed legislation to protect AT&T from competition at the urging and persistence of telephone industrialist Theodore Vail.

One Policy, One System, Universal Service

In 1907, Theodore Vail was appointed president of AT&T and publicly pushed his vision of a single telephone system through an advertising campaign and slogan, "One Policy, One System, Universal Service." At that time, the US government wanted more competition and was agitated when Vail began buying independent competitors and purchased telegraph giant Western Union, which gave AT&T a monopolistic position in both telegraph and telephones. In response, the government negotiated the Kingsbury Commitment with AT&T in 1913, in which AT&T agreed to divest Western Union, to provide long-distance services to independent local phone companies, and to refrain from acquisitions.

However, there was a loophole. Under the Commitment, AT&T was allowed to swap telephones with competitors. The result was AT&T and other operators swapped phones to create their own geographic monopolies and avoid price competition—contrary to the goal of the Commitment. The Commitment did reduce AT&T's ability to put competitors out of business—but it also deterred competitors from focusing outside their regional monopolies and attempting to build a competitive long-distance network. Legislators had designed the Commitment to be pro-competitive, but there were unintended consequences aplenty, and it had the opposite effect (which typically happens when it comes to major regulation or legislation).

Instead of feeling threatened by AT&T's monopolistic regional actions and the lack of competition in long-distance service, many legislators and regulators began to view a telephone monopoly as "natural"—likely due to Theodore Vail's public relations efforts. They thought (rightly or wrongly) competition resulted in duplication of investment and was therefore economically inefficient. Ultimately, for Vail and AT&T, it was more advantageous to be a heavily regulated monopoly than face the high and uncertain risks posed by competition.

While heavy government regulation and intervention are typically significant headwinds for most businesses, AT&T fared just fine.

Even during World War I, when AT&T was nationalized for a year for security reasons, prices weren't capped and it was even allowed to initiate a 20 percent hike in long-distance rates—a hike that remained in place for years after its re-privatization. Moreover, it's estimated AT&T retained approximately $42 million (84 percent) of the estimated $50 million ($723 million in 2010 dollars[9]) in rate increases approved by the government during nationalization. If that wasn't enough, the government then paid AT&T $13 million ($188 million in 2010 dollars[10]) to cover any losses the company may have incurred during nationalization, even though none were evident.[11]

The Communications Act of 1934 and Telecom Stability

After its re-privatization in 1919, AT&T operated as a monopoly with little regulatory interruption until the New Deal, when President Franklin D. Roosevelt sought to consolidate the regulation of all communications into one agency. By signing the Communications Act of 1934, Roosevelt created the Federal Communications Commission (FCC), which replaced the Federal Radio Commission and the Interstate Commerce Commission. The FCC was given power to impose service requirements at regulated rates in the Telecommunications sector and to control licensing and radio spectrum allocations—which effectively allowed it to regulate who entered the market. But while the Communications Act was part of the historically significant New Deal, it changed little for AT&T and instead nurtured a stable regulatory environment that secured AT&T's monopoly for decades.

The greater part of the twentieth century was relatively uneventful for the Telecom sector because AT&T dominated—it had approximately 90 percent of market share in long distance and local access lines. AT&T maximized its dominance and monopolistic powers by relying on its own Western Electric and Bell Laboratories subsidiaries. Almost all the equipment AT&T used was produced by Western Electric, and all its applied and theoretical research was conducted by its powerful Bell Laboratories, which has produced seven Nobel Prize winners and major inventions like the transistor.

Although regulators ostensibly aimed to protect citizens from monopolies, they also had incentive to protect AT&T because American businesses and society were dependent on its services. Nevertheless, antitrust lawsuits periodically flared up, and in 1949, the US Department of Justice (DOJ) claimed the Bell Operating Companies practiced illegal exclusion by buying production and premise equipment only from Western Electric. The DOJ sought a Western Electric divestment, but AT&T settled in 1956—retaining ownership of Western Electric and avoiding its breakup by agreeing not to enter the nascent computer market.

With little competition and no change to AT&T's businesses, its performance was much like other regulated utilities, such as gas and electric companies. Until significant legislation in 1996, Telecom overall performed similarly to the Utilities sector. As illustrated in Figure 2.1, between 1962 and 1996, Telecom outperformed the

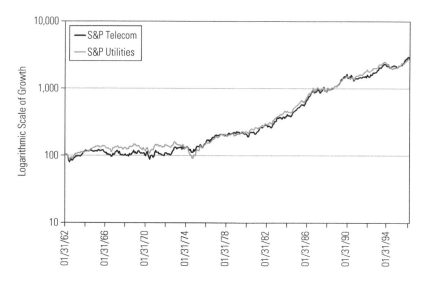

Figure 2.1   Telecom Versus Utilities Performance—Before Act of 1996

Source: Global Financial Data, Inc.; total returns for S&P Telecommunications and S&P 500 Composite, 02/28/62 to 02/29/96.

Telecommunications Antiques

Ticker tape. One of the earliest stock tickers was developed by Thomas Edison in 1869. Stock price information was sent via telegraph and printed approximately one character per second. Centuries later, the ticker tape lives on in the scrolling electronic tickers used by financial TV networks and financial institutions.

The pay phone. Superman would have a tough time finding a place to change these days—as recently as 1999, there were 1.8 million pay phones in the US. In 2008, there were just 420,000.[12]

The "Brick." The first commercially available cell phone, Motorola's DynaTAC 8000X, aka The Brick, came to market in 1983, cost $3,995, weighed almost two pounds, and offered 30 minutes of talk time.

Utilities sector by a paltry 6.5 percent—mere pennies over that time period—with a high correlation of 0.69.

RECENT HISTORY

It wasn't until the latter part of the twentieth century that Telecom regulation, and subsequently the competitive landscape, changed significantly. As a result, Telecom's and Utilities' relative performance deviated too. In stark contrast to Figure 2.1, Figure 2.2 shows between 1996 and 2009, Utilities outperformed the Telecom sector by 40 percent, and the correlation between the two sectors dropped to 0.26. The dramatic difference was driven by a string of events that began with an antitrust suit in 1974.

Ma Bell Has Septuplets

In 1974, the gig was up—both the DOJ and MCI (see the MCI Communications Corp. feature further on for more about MCI) filed antitrust suits against AT&T. AT&T dominated the local telephone network, which is needed to complete a long distance call, and it

Figure 2.2   Telecom Versus Utilities Performance—After Act of 1996

Source: Global Financial Data, Inc.; total returns for S&P Telecommunications and S&P 500 Composite, 02/29/96 to 10/31/09.

could favor its own long distance services over MCI's. The government alleged AT&T restricted competition in the Telecommunications market and therefore sought divestment of AT&T's long distance services and of its Western Electric unit—again. AT&T fought the case for years, but settled with the Federal District Court for the District of Columbia in 1982.

In 1984, the federal court-approved Modification of Final Judgment (MFJ) required AT&T (Ma Bell) to break up into eight pieces—seven Baby Bells and one AT&T. AT&T was the remaining long distance provider, plus Bell Labs research and its equipment businesses. The seven Baby Bells, or Regional Bell Operating Companies (RBOCs), were formed as a spin-off from AT&T's pre-existing 22 Bell operating companies. Each RBOC was effectively a regulated mini-monopoly that provided local services and was prohibited from providing long distance services.

By creating a division between AT&T's long distance and local networks, regulators succeeded in encouraging long distance competition,

MCI Communications Corp.

Technology has given rise to many new Telecom services and firms—one such company was MCI. In 1969, the upstart carrier won FCC approval to use newly developed
microwave technology to compete with AT&T. The technology enabled MCI to build its
own services between Chicago and St. Louis at a relatively low cost. The lower costs
associated with the new technology flew in the face of Telecom being a natural monopoly due to the economic inefficiencies of duplicating networks. MCI quickly obtained
permission to provide long-distance services, and AT&T was hit by a long-forgotten
foe—real competition.

and consumers benefited. Between 1984 and 2000, AT&T's long distance market share dropped from 90 percent to under 40 percent, and
the cost of making a long distance call dropped 70 percent![13] After
decades of little opposition and a stable regulatory environment, the
Telecom sector (at least the long distance market) began to look more
like a competitive market and less like a heavily regulated utility.

The Telecommunications Act of 1996

The 1984 breakup of Ma Bell was intended to increase competition
in the equipment and long distance markets, and later, the Telecommunications Act of 1996 sought to further increase competition—but
at the local level.

At the local level, carriers had been clamoring for ways to grow
their businesses and had been petitioning Congress to be allowed into
the long distance market. In 1996, their wishes came true—but with
a catch: Local carriers were allowed to enter long distance only after
they offered wholesale network access and network interconnection
opportunities to new competitors.

ILECs and CLECs The law detailed pricing formulas for both
wholesale network access and interconnection services. Wholesale

network prices charged by the Incumbent Local Exchange Carrier (ILEC) on the Competitive Local Exchange Carrier (CLEC) were set by the FCC at the federal level at cost plus a "reasonable profit." Those prices were then used by Public Utility Commissions at the state level to set local rates. The interconnection fees were based on a "reciprocal compensation" that assumed the average customer's calls would result in minimal net payments between carriers.

However, the regulated pricing wasn't as successful at promoting local competition because the Ma Bell breakup affected long distance services. As with a lot of regulation, it didn't have the impact initially sought. For many ILECs, the benefit of gaining access to the long distance market was less valuable than maintaining their regional monopolies, so they simply delayed opening their networks to competitors.

The Universal Service Fund   Universal service was initially promoted by Theodore Vail and the government as a rationale for AT&T's monopoly—they argued it would create a consistent technology that would make national network connections feasible. Over time, "universal" came to mean quality and reasonably priced services for all citizens.

As a result, the Telecommunications Act of 1996 created the Universal Service Fund (USF) to subsidize the costs of providing telecommunication services to largely rural and low-income populations. The significance for the Telecom sector is that some Telecom firms (aka telcos) receive subsidies to provide services, while the majority pay a percentage of their revenues to finance the USF. However, because contribution rates depend on how much money the USF believes it needs, the amounts can vary and the impact on telcos is difficult to predict.

Dot-coms and Seven Becomes Three

Despite some ILECs' unwillingness to open their networks to competitors, local and long distance competition increased in the late 1990s as investors started pouring money into the Telecom sector. CLECs and just about anything Telecom became hot investments because of recently lowered barriers to entry and because these companies were laying fiber optic cables—the backbone for the Internet economy. It was a brand-new world: Telecom was no longer a boring utility—it was finally sexy!

But it wouldn't last—although Telecom capital expenditures (building and upgrading networks) have always been cyclical, the dot-com bubble represented a boom-and-bust cycle the historically regulated sector had never before experienced.

High-flying companies like WorldCom and Global Crossing had both loaded up on debt to fund their spending—and collapsed. Even a giant like AT&T lost more than 50 percent of its market value.

The Great Consolidation   Even before the Tech bust caused many Telecom firms to disappear, the Telecom sector began consolidating in the mid-1990s due to fierce competition. Telecom firms have consolidated through mergers and acquisitions, as shown in Figure 2.3. While deregulation sought to increase competition by lowering barriers to entry and increasing the number of entrants, the reality has been companies must consolidate to compete—just three of the original seven Baby Bells are left.

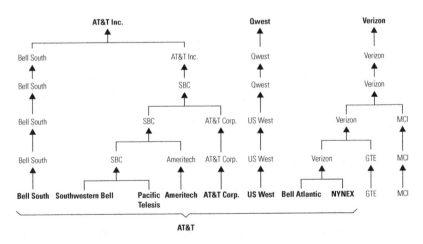

Figure 2.3   Sector Consolidation: Mid 1990s–2007

Chapter Recap

The past provides context for analyzing the present and attempting to predict the future. The sector transformed from an idea many considered a passing novelty to one of the world's most important services.

Despite the significant changes throughout the sector's history, there are trends that may lend some insight into the sector's future:

- For much of the last century, high costs to provide telecommunication services resulted in significant sector regulation and protectionism.

- However, as new technologies have driven telecommunication costs down, regulation has decreased and competition has increased, resulting in lower prices and more services for consumers.

- As a heavily regulated sector, Telecom behaved like the Utilities sector prior to the mid-1990s. But since then, deregulation, competition, and the Internet bubble (and burst) have caused Telecom's performance to be more volatile and sensitive to the ups and downs of the economic cycle.

3

TELECOM SECTOR COMPOSITION

Y ou should now understand Telecom basics and have reviewed the sector's historical development. In this chapter, we'll examine how the Telecom sector fits into the global stock market, review the different industries that make up the sector, and take a peek at some of the sector's biggest companies. Establishing the sector's composition will provide a structure we can build upon. It lays the foundation for business drivers in Part II and is a blueprint for portfolio construction in Part III.

GLOBAL INDUSTRY CLASSIFICATION STANDARD (GICS)

We've talked a lot about *sectors* and a little about *industries* thus far, so before we go any further, let's define exactly what we mean. The Global Industry Classification Standard (GICS) is a widely accepted framework for classifying companies into groups based on similarities. The GICS structure consists of 10 sectors, 24 industry groups,

68 industries, and 154 sub-industries. This structure offers four levels of hierarchy:

- Sector
- Industry group
- Industry
- Sub-industry

The Telecom sector is narrowly focused on communication services and has a much simpler hierarchy than most sectors, with just one industry group, two industries, and three sub-industries. Telecom's industries and corresponding sub-industries are:

Industry: Diversified Telecommunication Services

- Sub-industry: Integrated Telecommunication Services
- Sub-industry: Alternative Carriers

Industry: Wireless Telecommunication Services

- Sub-industry: Wireless Telecommunication Services

Before delving deeper into the industries, it's vital to understand what the Telecom sector looks like globally and how it fits into a broader benchmark.

GLOBAL TELECOM BENCHMARKS

What's a benchmark? What does it do, and why is it necessary? Simply, a benchmark is your guide for building a stock portfolio. It's a point of reference—a standard for measurement and evaluation, and an investor's roadmap for building a stock portfolio. You can use any well-constructed index—like the MSCI World or S&P 500, for example—as a benchmark. This is just as true for a sector as it is for the broader stock market. And by studying the index's composition, you can assign expected risk and return to make underweight

Table 3.1   Benchmark Comparison

	MSCI ACWI	MSCI World	MSCI EM	MSCI EAFE	MSCI Eurozone	S&P 500 Composite	Russell 2000
Financials	21.1%	20.7%	25.5%	25.2%	25.2%	16.5%	20.1%
Information Technology	12.0%	11.9%	13.0%	5.1%	4.6%	18.8%	18.1%
Energy	11.1%	10.7%	13.9%	8.0%	7.9%	10.8%	5.4%
Industrials	10.2%	10.6%	7.1%	11.6%	11.1%	10.6%	16.2%
Consumer Staples	9.8%	10.4%	6.5%	10.3%	9.2%	11.3%	3.7%
Health Care	9.3%	10.3%	0.8%	8.6%	6.2%	12.1%	12.8%
Consumer Discretionary	9.0%	9.5%	6.7%	9.7%	9.2%	10.1%	14.3%
Materials	8.3%	7.3%	14.4%	10.1%	8.2%	3.5%	5.0%
Telecommunication Services	**4.8%**	**4.2%**	**8.3%**	**5.7%**	**8.3%**	**2.8%**	**1.2%**
Utilities	4.3%	4.4%	3.8%	5.8%	10.1%	3.4%	3.2%

Source: Thomson Reuters, as of 12/31/09.

and overweight decisions for each category. (We'll talk more about benchmarks in Chapter 7.)

So what does the Telecom investment universe look like? It depends on the benchmark. Table 3.1 shows seven indexes with the weight of each of the 10 market sectors. All of the indexes, except for the S&P 500 Composite, are *float-adjusted* (i.e., they exclude shares held by the government). The broadest benchmark is the MSCI All-Country World Index (ACWI)—which includes both developed and Emerging Markets (EM). The MSCI World includes only developed countries; the EAFE, only developed foreign countries; and the Eurozone is what it sounds like. The S&P 500 and Russell 2000 are specific to the United States and United States small cap stocks, respectively.

Why Doesn't Telecom Have More Weight?

Telecom is clearly one of the smallest sectors in the global stock market. But how can a sector that plays such a fundamental role in the global economy be such a small part of the investment universe? There are two primary reasons:

- Telecom is a relatively small part of the global economy—it's approximately 3 percent of the Organisation of Economic Co-operation and Development's (OECD, a group of 33 developed countries) GDP.[1]
- There aren't many publicly traded Telecom stocks to choose from because of high government ownership, heavy regulation, and high fixed costs.

Benchmark Differences

Though Telecom tends to be a small portion of the broadest equity benchmarks, the sector is a major portion of some regional markets. Table 3.2 shows MSCI Telecom weightings in selected countries. Telecom weightings vary greatly, based on the region's market

Table 3.2   Telecom Weights by Country

Country	Telecom Weight in MSCI All Country World Index
New Zealand	27.6%
Egypt	26.6%
Spain	25.0%
Portugal	23.7%
Philippines	21.0%
Czech Republic	19.0%
Austria	14.0%
Indonesia	13.4%
China	13.0%
South Africa	12.8%
Singapore	11.9%
Turkey	11.4%
Malaysia	11.2%
Hungary	10.5%

Country	Telecom Weight in MSCI All Country World Index
Sweden	9.9%
Israel	8.8%
Poland	8.4%
Belgium	7.6%
Russia	7.1%
United Kingdom	7.1%
Greece	6.2%
Italy	6.2%
Thailand	5.3%
Germany	5.0%
Taiwan	4.6%
France	4.1%
Japan	4.0%
United States	3.2%
Canada	2.9%
Chile	2.9%
Korea	2.9%
Brazil	2.6%
Finland	2.6%
Australia	1.6%
Switzerland	1.2%
India	0.8%
Hong Kong	0.5%

Source: Thomson Reuters, as of 12/31/09.

liberalization and the number of other country holdings in the index. The wide range is exemplified by two neighboring islands, New Zealand and Australia. Telecom New Zealand, which was separated from the Post Office and then privatized, is a whopping 27.6 percent of the country weighting. Telstra, formerly Telecom Australia and similarly separated from the Post Office and then privatized, is only 1.6 percent of its country weighting. Whereas there are only 5 companies in the New Zealand benchmark and Telecom New Zealand is the largest, there are 71 in the Australian benchmark and Telstra is scrawny compared to mining giants like BHP Billiton.[2]

Understanding how benchmarks are structured is crucial to developing a portfolio because of the wide deviations in sector weights. For example, if you put 5 percent of your portfolio in Telecom, you would be significantly underweight relative to a New Zealand benchmark, but you'd be overweight relative to an Australian benchmark.

Benchmark Changes

Benchmark composition isn't fixed and can change over time due to performance differences, additions, and deletions of companies in the index, plus a variety of other factors. The potential volatility of a benchmark weighting is illustrated in Figure 3.1. Due largely to the explosive share performance of the Telecom sector in the late 1990s, its weight in the global stock market was almost three times its current weighting!

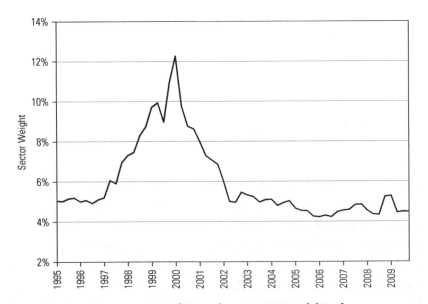

Figure 3.1   Telecom Weight in the MSCI World Index
Source: Thomson Reuters, MSCI ACWI Index, 1995–2009.

As benchmarks change, investors may need to adjust their port-folios just to maintain stable relative overweight and underweight allocations.

Sector Benchmarks

Just like the broader market, sectors have their own benchmarks, and each industry constitutes a portion of the overall Telecom bench-mark. And just like the broader market, investors may overweight and underweight different categories based on their expected risk and return characteristics. Table 3.3 shows the weight of each industry and sub-industry for seven different Telecom benchmarks.

With the exception of Emerging Markets, Diversified Services is the dominant benchmark weighting due to Integrated Services compa-nies. Integrated Services consists of the huge fixed-line monopolies or government-owned companies that were privatized (like AT&T). Today, such companies are often a mix of both fixed-line and wireless services.

Whereas Integrated Services companies can do just about any-thing, Wireless Services companies concentrate only on wireless. Wireless Services has a larger weight in the Emerging Markets bench-mark because of generally high government ownership in fixed-line

Table 3.3   Industry and Sub-Industry Weights by Benchmark

	MSCI ACWI	MSCI World	MSCI EM	MSCI EAFE	MSCI Eurozone	S&P 500 Composite*	Russell 2000 Small Cap
Diversified Services	**61%**	**70%**	**27%**	**65%**	**99%**	**89%**	**72%**
Integrated Services	60%	69%	26%	63%	98%	—	28%
Alternative Carriers	1%	1%	1%	2%	1%	—	44%
Wireless Services	**39%**	**30%**	**73%**	**35%**	**1%**	**11%**	**28%**

*S&P 500 does not break out Diversified Services at the sub-industry level.

Source: Thomson Reuters, as of 12/31/09.

providers and the rapid deployment of wireless technologies. In many developing regions, companies have elected to bypass the costs and time to lay fixed lines because those areas typically lack the infrastructure of the developed world. It is much cheaper and quicker to build a network of wireless towers than to string phone lines everywhere.

INDUSTRY BREAKDOWN

Now that you've got a sense of what the sector looks like at a high level, we can take a look at some of the distinguishing characteristics of its industry and sub-industry categories. We'll cover some of the basics here and then drill much deeper in Chapters 4 through 6 to understand what really drives the businesses and share prices.

Diversified Telecommunication Services

This industry is composed of two sub-industries: Integrated Services and Alternative Carriers. We focus almost entirely on the former because the latter is only a puny piece of almost all benchmarks. If you have a global portfolio with an approximate 5 percent weight to Telecom and you want to be in line with benchmark weightings, just 0.05 percent of your investments should be in Alternative Carriers—they're small potatoes.

Integrated Services These are the big boys. The 10 largest Diversified Services firms are listed in Table 3.4, and they're all Integrated firms—not one is an Alternative Carrier. In fact, there's not one Alternative in the top 30. Although AT&T still boasts a huge market cap, it has fallen from its perch as the world's largest corporation. Like many of its peers, it started in the fixed-line business. But because fixed line is a mature product with few growth opportunities, many traditional fixed-line providers (AT&T included) have ventured into wireless, broadband, TV, and foreign geographies to grow their bottom line.

It's worth concentrating on Integrated Services bellwethers like AT&T because how they perform will dictate how the industry

Table 3.4   Ten Largest Diversified Services Companies

Name	Country	Market Capitalization (USD Billions)	% Weight in Industry
AT&T	USA	165,405	21.3%
Telefonica	Spain	127,817	13.0%
Verizon Communications	USA	94,111	11.5%
France Telecom	France	66,233	5.4%
Deutsche Telekom	Germany	64,387	5.3%
Nippon Telg. & Tel.	Japan	61,717	3.0%
Telstra	Australia	38,383	1.8%
Singapore Telecom	Singapore	35,289	2.5%
TeliaSonera	Sweden	32,609	2.3%
China Unicom	China	31,238	1.1%

Source: Thomson Reuters, MSCI ACWI Index as of 12/31/09.[3]

performs and give you a better understanding of broad trends and investment themes. Integrated Services is concentrated—the top five companies in the MSCI ACWI account for 57 percent of its benchmark weight.[4]

Alternative Carriers   MSCI defines this group as providers of communications and high-density data transmission services primarily through a high bandwidth or fiber-optic cable network. It's a small list made up of a hodgepodge of companies—the major satellite and cable firms that provide communication services also provide television services and are therefore categorized in the Consumer Discretionary sector. Although they are relatively small, the leading Alternative Carrier companies are Inmarsat (a British satellite company) and Iliad (a French company that offers broadband, traditional phone services, and insurance policies online).

Wireless Telecommunication Services

The providers of cellular and wireless services, including paging services, have grown in importance and weight in the Telecom sector.

Table 3.5   Ten Largest Wireless Service Companies

Name	Country	Market Capitalization (USD Billions)	% Weight in Industry
China Mobile	China	188,473	13.1%
Vodafone Group	UK	122,078	26.4%
NTT Docomo	Japan	61,184	5.2%
America Movil	Mexico	47,443	10.1%
MTN Group	South Africa	29,469	5.7%
Softbank	Japan	25,232	5.2%
KDDI	Japan	23,750	3.0%
Mobile Telesystems	Russia	19,491	2.4%
American Tower	USA	17,347	4.0%
Turkcell	Turkey	15,558	1.0%

Source: Thomson Reuters; MSCI Inc.,[6] MSCI ACWI Index as of 12/31/09.

Falling prices for handsets and minutes have made wireless services affordable for billions of consumers and given rise to billionaires like Carlos Slim—CEO of America Movil, Telmex, and Telcel, and one of the wealthiest men in the world.

Similar to the Diversified Services industry, Wireless' weighting is concentrated in the top five bellwethers, which account for 61 percent of the benchmark[5]—see Table 3.5. Unlike Diversified firms, numerous leading Wireless firms are in developing countries. Traditional wireline businesses may not be as big in developing countries, and in many cases, the wireless business is separate from the incumbent wireline provider. The US and some other countries are different. For example, AT&T and Verizon are leaders in both wireless and wireline services—because they offer both, they're categorized in the Diversified category.

A US company that did make the Wireless list is American Tower. While most Wireless companies provide wireless services to consumers, tower companies are a little different—instead of selling directly to consumers, they lease space on their towers to service providers.

> ### Large Market Cap, but Small Float
>
> Compared to Vodafone, note in Table 3.5 what a small percentage China Mobile contributes to the industry weight relative to its market capitalization—a good example of a small float due to large government ownership. As a state-owned enterprise, China Mobile benefits from a certain level of government protection, but its bottom line can also be hampered by government action to make phones available and affordable for all citizens.

SAME, SAME, BUT DIFFERENT

The GICS Telecommunication sector contains just three sub-industries. They are companies that provide communications services primarily through a fixed-line, wireless, cellular, and high bandwidth and/or fiber optic cable. That leaves out competing Cable & Satellite companies like Comcast and Time Warner (found in the Consumer Discretionary sector) and Communications Equipment companies like Cisco and Nokia (located in the Information Technology sector) that make routers, switches, phones, and the other equipment used for communications. If you thought you'd play the iPhone popularity and buy Apple as a Telecom company, think again—it's in the Computers & Peripherals industry, which falls under the Information Technology sector.

Chapter Recap

In order to understand what drives the Telecom sector and how to build a portfolio, we have started with the sector's composition. We use the Global Industry Classification Standard (GICS), a widely accepted framework for classifying companies into groups based on similarities, to structure the sector's composition. The GICS structure consists of 10 sectors, 24 industry groups, 68 industries, and 154 sub-industries.

- The Telecom sector has a simple structure—it's composed of just the Diversified Services and Wireless Services industries and three sub-industries.

(Continued)

- Diversified Services has two sub-industries: Integrated Services and Alternative Carriers.

- Integrated Services is the bulk of the industry weighting and includes companies like AT&T—the huge, traditional telephone companies that, in many instances, have expanded into wireless, broadband, and TV. Bellwethers like AT&T often provide insight into broad Telecom trends and investment themes.

- Alternative Carriers are generally composed of an assortment of cable and satellite companies that offer communication services, but not television. Alternatives are such a small part of Diversified Services' weight, even a small portfolio position would likely represent an overweight relative to common benchmarks.

- Due to declining prices and expansive availability, the Wireless Services subindustry growth has been robust in both developed and emerging markets. Wireless services enable emerging markets to bypass many of the costs and much of the time needed to develop an extensive fixed-line infrastructure.

II

NEXT STEPS:
TELECOM DETAILS

4

TELECOM
SECTOR DRIVERS

F irst of all, what is a driver? Drivers are factors that impact—positively or negatively—the performance of stocks, industries, sectors, and the entire market. In this chapter, we'll look at how drivers impact the performance of Telecom—both the broad category and individual stocks—relative to the benchmark.

There are three broad categories of drivers you can use to examine the forward-looking prospects for any stock market sector:

1. Economic Drivers
2. Political Drivers
3. Sentiment Drivers

Drivers—in any of these categories—impact Telecom's relative performance in a variety of ways: They may affect earnings, profitability, growth, cost of capital, industry regulations, and investors' appetite for risk, among other things. But investors should primarily be concerned about how drivers ultimately impact investment returns relative to the broader market.

As you learn about drivers in this chapter, it's important to remember the relative importance of different drivers varies throughout time—this is especially true in Telecom, which has undergone significant structural changes and become much more competitive as deregulation has progressed globally. Often, different drivers point in different directions, and it is up to investors to determine which drivers are most important at any given point.

ECONOMIC DRIVERS

A full book could easily be devoted to economic drivers, but this section will focus on the macroeconomic drivers most applicable to the Telecom sector, which include:

- Economic growth (or lack thereof)
- Interest rates
- Inflation
- Innovation

The easiest way to measure economic drivers is through a slew of macroeconomic indicators that are publicly released regularly. Macroeconomic indicators take the pulse of the economy. Countries' gross domestic product (GDP) numbers, interest rates, and inflation help paint a picture of the current state of the economy. And they can help you shape expectations about the economy and how it may impact telcos looking forward. Deciphering economic data isn't easy. Economic reports can be volatile, contradict one another, and are often subject to later revisions. And economic data are usually inherently backward-looking. The data report on what just happened; they don't necessarily tell you what is going to happen. Markets discount economic news with astounding speed, so investors need to know more than what happened—they must consider what's next.

So how do you use macroeconomic data to your advantage? By staying abreast of the most important indicators and asking whether present conditions are better or worse than what's reflected in investor sentiment and market prices. Then, consider where you think the economy is most likely to go in the future based on current trends. You're looking for predictive value. You're not as interested in what's on the cover of the *Wall Street Journal* today. You're interested in what's going to be on the cover next month or next year.

Economic Growth

As a defensive sector with limited sensitivity to the economic cycle (see Chapter 1), Telecom tends to perform best relative to the rest of the stock market when the economic outlook is weakening. This is not because a weak economy is actually beneficial for Telecom fundamentals—after all, employment and housing construction drive demand for fixed lines, and consumer spending affects mobile phone revenue. It's just that Telecom is less economically sensitive than most other sectors. As such, it's seen as a relatively safer bet than more economically sensitive sectors (like Energy, Materials, and Consumer Discretionary) when expectations are for weaker growth.

The most frequently used measure of economic growth is gross domestic product—the aggregate output of an economy. But quarterly GDP data are released a month after the quarter ends—they are inherently backward-looking. By the time quarterly GDP is published, economists have already reviewed a plethora of weekly and monthly data releases, and the general economic trend is usually fairly well discounted by the stock market.

And because the stock market tends to lead the economy, Telecom's relative performance tends to be more closely negatively correlated with some leading indicators of the economy rather than with GDP itself. One indicator that's historically been useful is the Institute for Supply Management's Purchasing Manager's Index—or PMI (www.ism.ws). This index is based on a survey of purchasing managers at manufacturing firms in the United States and gauges the direction of the industrial economy, including trends in new orders, production, shipments, employment, pricing, and other metrics. A rising PMI is a fairly good indicator of increasing economic activity, while a falling PMI is typically indicative of a slowing or shrinking economy.

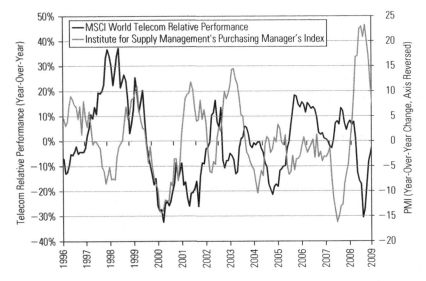

Figure 4.1   Telecom Relative Performance and the Purchasing Manager's Index

Sources: Thomson Reuters, MSCI World Telecommunication Services and MSCI World Index total returns;[1] Institute for Supply Management, Purchasing Managers Index, 8/15/96 to 8/15/10.

Figure 4.1 shows the trailing one-year return of the MSCI World Telecom Index relative to the MSCI World (left axis), and the year-over-year-change in the PMI (right axis). Telecom has historically outperformed when the PMI index is falling and underperformed when it is rising. However, one major exception was at the turn of the twenty-first century, when both the PMI and Telecom deflated with the Tech bubble (which we covered in Chapter 2).

Interest Rates

Telecom's performance, relative to the broad market, has historically demonstrated a negative correlation to the 10-year US Treasury yield—a benchmark for the risk-free interest rate. When a bear market hits, investors are scared and often flee to investments deemed safe and defensive. So they buy Telecom stocks because their revenue and earnings are typically more stable than more economically sensitive sectors. Simultaneously, investors tend to favor US Treasuries because they are considered "risk-free." Such buying drives the prices of bonds up and their yields down. Also, yields fall because the Federal Reserve usually lowers its discount rate during a bear market, which pressures Treasury yields down and provides banks more incentive to lend and help reignite economic growth. The net effect is that when interest rates are going down, it may be a good time to overweight Telecom.

Telecom benefits not just from stock investors seeking shelter in a bear market, but also from fixed-income investors seeking a yield. US Treasury yields get driven so low, investors can be attracted to Telecom's relatively high dividend yield.

Lastly, Telecom outperforms when interest rates are low because it's capital intensive and firms are highly dependent on bond markets for long-term financing. When interest rates are high and credit is tight, Telecom firms have to pay much more in interest—which can be a drag on earnings. Not only does it cost more to fund current debt, but without access to more money, spending will likely decrease—which could slow growth in the near term.

Just as Telecom tends to outperform when interest rates are falling, it typically underperforms when rates are rising for the same reasons. Rising interest rates usually coincide with bull markets, when economically sensitive stocks are in favor—that's typically when Telecom's dividend yield is relatively unattractive and when firms' interest expenses are high and tend to weigh on earnings.

If you have a firm conviction on which direction you think interest rates will go, you may want to overweight or underweight Telecom accordingly.

Inflation

Expectations for higher inflation are generally bad for Telecom and a signal to underweight the sector. Why? Interest rates again—inflationary periods usually coincide with high interest rates.

When inflation expectations rise, lenders require higher nominal interest rates on loans in order to maintain their real (i.e., inflation-adjusted) rate of return. And historically, the yield on the 10-year Treasury note tends to track inflation expectations.

Nevertheless, inflation is a good example of how tricky it can be to interpret whether an economic driver is pointing to Telecom outperforming or underperforming the broader market. Some argue inflation is good for Telecom firms because regulatory mechanisms allow them to pass along rising costs more easily than other sectors, which results in their outperformance. And while Telecom tends to underperform more often than not during periods of expected higher inflation, it's important to remember there will always be exceptions.

Innovation

Innovation of new technologies cannot be overlooked as an important driver of the Telecom sector. Consider the transition from analog to digital transmissions and the cost reductions and deregulation that has accompanied it—innovation has reshaped the Telecom landscape, with significant impacts for investors.

There is no easy way to forecast innovation or to anticipate the speed at which it transforms the sector—for better or worse—but investors who see the promise of new technologies in their earliest stages and can correctly understand how it will impact Telecom may have an advantage over others. This is true on the sector level, but also on the industry and stock level—more innovative players are likely to be better relative bets.

Today, Telecom is facing the rapid development of new technologies and services, but it isn't always clear what future supply and demand will be and what prices consumers will be willing to pay. Although it is widely known that smartphones increase data consumption, few correctly predicted the wild popularity of Apple's iPhone—or the stress it would put on AT&T's network when data usage suddenly spiked. When it's tough to predict demand, it's tough to predict supply. For example, during the Tech craze of the late 1990s, wild estimates for Internet growth rates drove telcos to grossly overinvest in bandwidth—then subsequently get slaughtered when the growth projections turned out to be wrong. CEOs may be cautious about repeating a mistake they so recently made.

POLITICAL DRIVERS

Government policies are used around the world to stimulate or slow economic activity (with varying degrees of success), redistribute wealth, promote social goals, or simply generate tax revenue. Although the net societal benefits of any new government policy are usually a matter of perspective, most policy changes do create economic winners and losers.

Government policy affects the Telecom sector in many ways, ranging from expansive changes, like net neutrality (which we'll discuss in Chapter 6), that could affect a broad array of industries and practically all consumers, to local regulatory proceedings that affect only a regional carrier. Some of the most important political drivers affecting the Telecom sector include:

- Political shifts
- Regulatory changes

Political Shifts

It's not always easy to predict what regulation will be passed and enforced by a political administration. After all, who could have predicted Janet Jackson's "wardrobe malfunction" during the halftime show of Super Bowl XXXVIII would kickstart a chain of events leading to President George W. Bush signing a law that stiffened decency penalties from $32,500 to $325,000 per violation?

Under most political administrations, regulators ostensibly seek to protect consumers—but what they're being protected from can differ. Under the Bush administration, the FCC protected consumers from "wardrobe malfunctions," while the Obama administration seeks to protect consumers from industry misbehavior through net neutrality.

In most markets, deregulation spurs cheaper prices, innovation, and greater competition and investment, which can benefit consumers, investors, and companies. With this in mind, one might hypothesize Telecom performs better when elections bring Republican governments to power (which tend to favor less government involvement

Table 4.1   Telecom and US Presidential Administrations

Presidential Term	Start Date	End Date	Party	S&P Telecom	S&P 500 Composite	Telecom Relative Return
John F. Kennedy	1961	1963	D	36.5%	39.3%	−2.8%
Lyndon B. Johnson	1963	1965	D	7.6%	18.6%	−11.0%
Lyndon B. Johnson	1965	1969	D	−5.9%	39.0%	−44.8%
Richard M. Nixon	1969	1973	R	21.4%	29.4%	−8.0%
Richard M. Nixon	1973	1974	R	−15.9%	−29.0%	13.1%
Gerald R. Ford	1974	1977	R	79.1%	50.4%	28.7%
Jimmy Carter	1977	1981	D	6.2%	55.5%	−49.3%
Ronald Reagan	1981	1985	R	125.2%	50.5%	74.7%
Ronald Reagan	1985	1989	R	124.2%	91.8%	32.4%
George Bush	1989	1993	R	73.0%	79.2%	−6.2%
William J. Clinton	1993	1997	D	57.6%	88.7%	−31.0%
William J. Clinton	1997	2001	D	56.9%	88.7%	−31.8%
George W. Bush	2001	2005	R	−25.8%	−2.1%	−23.7%
George W. Bush	2005	2009	R	0.5%	−19.3%	19.7%
Republican Presidential Terms Average				**47.7%**	**31.4%**	**16.3%**
Democratic Presidential Terms Average				**26.5%**	**54.9%**	**−28.5%**
Overall Average				**38.6%**	**41.5%**	**−2.9%**

Source: Global Financial Data, Inc., total returns for S&P 500 Telecommunication Services and S&P 500 Composite, 1961–2009.

in the sector)—and worse under Democratic governments (which have often advocated for a larger government role). As illustrated in Table 4.1, this does seem to be the case: Telecom has performed better on both a relative and absolute basis under Republican governments. The table shows returns for the Telecom sector and the S&P 500, the Telecom sector's relative return for each presidential term, and the average returns during both Republican and Democratic terms since 1961.

But investors shouldn't draw too many conclusions about the future based on this historical analysis. The reality is a candidate's political affiliation and campaign promises tell us little about what his actual policy agenda might look like when he's in office—and even less about what he'll actually be able to accomplish. Politicians frequently say one thing and do another.

Moreover, there are many other factors at play that may be much more important than the political party in the White House. A large portion of Telecom's relative performance advantage during Republican administrations is the result of a weaker overall market—a trend that has been shown to be more attributable to longer-term cyclical trends than any specific public policy agenda.

So while elections—and the parties they bring to power—may provide a place to start political analysis, investors must ask deeper questions. What policies are on the legislative agenda? What do policymakers have to gain or lose from various political outcomes? Are there elections coming up that may have an impact? What do public opinion polls say about relevant issues? Who have policymakers appointed to implement and enforce their policies?

But even when the laws are passed and the rules are made, they don't always have the effect politicians intend—and sometimes they do almost the opposite. For example, as detailed in Chapter 2, the US government broke up Ma Bell to encourage more entrants and greater competition, but the opposite occurred. Since then, in order to better compete, the US Telecom sector has consolidated—of the original seven Baby Bells, only three remain.

The key to understanding a political agenda's impact is often determining the likelihood of whether regulation will be tightened or loosened—because it's surprises that move markets, not information that is already widely known.

Regulatory Changes

Transforming telecommunications from monopolies to competitive markets has required government intervention to ensure the monopolies don't behead new entrants and competition actually takes hold.

As the Telecom sector continues to liberalize, reconciling the interests of governments, customers, new entrants, and incumbents is challenging because they are often at odds. As a result, regulators have to make trade-offs between the objectives and welfare of different interest groups, which are often prioritized depending on the political party in power.

Regulation's Implementation

Although regulators' objectives (listed in Chapter 1) are usually widely accepted, their implementation is often controversial. Over the past couple decades, regulation has become more difficult as slow-moving government regulators try to keep pace with technological advancements and changing market dynamics. Whereas regulators previously monitored a voice business over one infrastructure, they now oversee voice, broadband, and video—and all three can be bundled together over various infrastructures. In such an environment, how regulation is implemented poses opportunities and risks to Telecom firms.

Pricing   Because monopolies or service providers with few competitors could charge high rates if unregulated, regulators attempt to emulate the outcomes of competitive markets to determine "fair" prices. There are numerous forms of price regulation in Telecom, but price caps are the most widely used. Price cap regulation uses a predetermined formula to set the price increases a firm can charge—usually for a couple years. Although the caps can be based on anything, they are often based either on inflation or costs. However, the caps can be controversial due to complications in calculating costs and the large impact they can have on both carriers and consumers.

And while price caps seem like a negative for telcos and Telecom investors, they can actually prove somewhat positive if a telco is allowed to keep any benefits from incremental productivity gains. Also, a price cap may encourage a company to seek more innovative services to bolster its business and shareholder value.

Nevertheless, price regulation exemplifies the difficulty of finding an optimal regulatory policy. Price controls may keep prices low for consumers, but they often deter competition and therefore contradict a primary goal for regulators. For example, when a regulator caps the price a telco can charge for a service, it not only hurts the operator who has less incentive to invest in its business, but may also deter new entrants and therefore competition. If prices are too low and new entrants are unable to recoup their high capital investments, they won't enter the market—so regulators must seek to set prices that ensure affordability for the public while allowing enough profitability for service providers to be motivated to reinvest in their businesses and for competitors to be motivated to enter the market.

Intercarrier Compensation   Interconnection or termination fees are the charges one telecommunications operator charges another for connecting and terminating calls on its network. For example, if you're an AT&T mobile customer and you call someone on Verizon Wireless, AT&T must pay a fee to Verizon. If you have ever been hit with a nasty mobile phone bill for roaming, interconnection fees were likely the culprit. Such interconnection fees can contribute significantly to a telco's bottom line and are therefore subject to considerable political risk. Take Turkcell, the largest wireless provider in Turkey. Regulators cut termination rates by 52 percent in 2010, which was great for customers and competitors, but terrible for Turkcell because it terminates disproportionately more calls on its network than on competitors'. As telecom markets have progressively liberalized, interconnection arrangements have become a critical factor for the viability of competition.

Licensing   Licenses are a way regulators can control the number of operators in a region and affect competition. In order to operate in the Telecommunications sector, licenses for new entrants are usually granted by the regulator through a competitive application process. Licenses not only regulate the level of competition in a market, but also provide investors an understanding of the business they are investing in—they specify what a company can and cannot do.

Spectrum Spectrum is another control governments and regulators have to dictate the level of supply and competition in a market. Governments control the availability and cost of radio frequency spectrum wireless providers operate on.

Taxes Tax policy is capable of materially impacting any company, and broad changes in the corporate tax rate have a direct effect on all companies' income. However, many changes aren't sweeping revisions to the tax code—they are typically smaller provisions that may go relatively unnoticed, but still may be important drivers.

Because the sector tends to return a large portion of its earnings to shareholders through dividends, changes in the dividend tax rate are particularly important to Telecom. In other words, the high dividend yields on Telecom stocks are worth more to investors on an after-tax basis when dividend taxes are lower.

SENTIMENT DRIVERS

Sentiment is the least tangible sector driver. Put simply, sentiment can mean how receptive people are to buying or selling stock—and like any mood, sentiment can change quickly and be hard to measure. It plays a large role in near-term market prices because the stock market is driven by humans making decisions—inclusive of their rational choices and their irrational emotions.

Risk Aversion

Perhaps the most important sentiment driver is risk aversion. Risk aversion can be so low or high, it causes investors to lose sight of economic and political drivers. Because of its defensive nature, Telecom tends to do better when investors are highly risk averse. When investors expect a bear market—rightly or wrongly—they tend to flock to the relative safety of Telecom.

Value Versus Growth

Growth investors tend to favor companies with above-average earnings growth rates, while value investors tend to prefer companies with below-average valuations. There are many benchmarks for these disciplines, including the well-known Russell Value and Growth indexes.

Although proponents of each style would argue their discipline is superior, the risk and return characteristics of both investment styles are similar over the long run. However, they do cycle in and out of favor. At times, growth steadily beats value, and at other times, value steadily beats growth.

Telecom, with its normally low growth rates and below-average valuations, tends to be shunned by growth investors and embraced by value investors. This is well illustrated in Figure 4.2, which shows the year-over-year return of US Telecom relative to the S&P 500 and

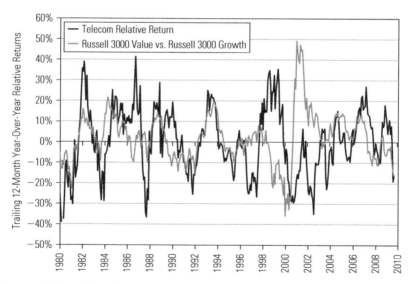

Figure 4.2   US Telecom Returns Relative to S&P 500 and Value-Growth Cycles

Source: Thomson Reuters, S&P 500 Composite total returns, Russell 3000 Value total returns, Russell 3000 Growth returns, 1979–2009; Global Financial Data, Inc., S&P 500 Telecommunication Services Index total returns, 1978–2009.

year-over-year return of the Russell 3000 Value relative to the Russell 3000 Growth. Because there is a fairly strong positive relationship, if you believe value stocks will be in favor and you're right, it's likely Telecom will outperform.

Large Cap Versus Small Cap

Similar to the value-growth cycle, there are periods in which companies with large market capitalizations (large cap) are favored over small capitalization (small cap) stocks and vice versa. Historically, big companies fare better during recessions while small companies bounce big early in the recovery. During periods of volatility and uncertainty, large companies are frequently seen as a relatively safer haven—they're seen as being stable businesses with healthier balance sheets that can weather an economic storm better than small companies. In turn, coming out of a recession, small cap stocks typically outperform

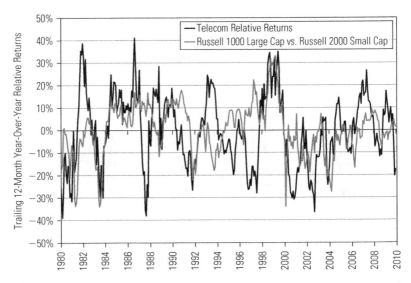

Figure 4.3   US Telecom Returns Relative to the S&P 500 Index and Large-Small Cap Cycles

Sources: Thomson Reuters, S&P 500 Composite total returns, Russell 1000 Index total returns, Russell 2000 Index total returns, 1979–2009; Global Financial Data, Inc., S&P 500 Telecommunication Services Index total returns, 1979–2009.

because they usually suffered more during the recession and bounce bigger off the bottom. They are seen as being more nimble and able to make strategic changes more quickly. They can also disproportionately benefit from an increase in mergers and acquisitions—which is common toward the end of a recession. (Though these characterizations of big versus small can certainly be true, perception is what's most powerful in driving stock returns in the near term.) And because telcos are usually huge, it's no surprise they typically perform better when large cap is beating small cap, as shown in Figure 4.3.

Chapter Recap

Like every other sector, Telecom has a set of economic, political, and sentiment drivers. Identifying these drivers can help determine when to overweight and underweight the Telecom sector. The relative importance of different drivers varies over time, and they often point in different directions. It's therefore up to you, the investor, to determine which drivers are most important at any given point.

- Telecom performs best relative to the rest of the stock market when the economic outlook is weakening. This is not because a weak economy is actually beneficial for Telecom fundamentals; it's just less detrimental than it is for most other sectors.

- Telecom tends to outperform when interest rates are falling and underperform when interest rates are rising.

- Because Telecom is regulated more than most sectors, the political and regulatory risks can be significant. Therefore, understanding political agendas can help investors predict potential regulatory changes and their impact on the sector.

- Risk aversion is the most important sentiment driver. Telecom tends to perform best when investors are highly risk averse.

- Telecom typically outperforms when value and/or large cap stocks are in favor.

5

CONSUMER DEMAND

The progression of this book has mimicked the top-down method of investing (detailed in Chapter 7). We began with the big picture (basics, history, and sector composition) and then moved on to drivers. The material so far should help investors decide whether to overweight or underweight the Telecom sector versus a benchmark for the next 12 to 18 months.

The purpose of the next two chapters is to facilitate both industry and stock-specific decisions. With economic, political, and sentiment drivers anchoring sector knowledge, you can sharpen your analysis by examining consumer demand trends in this chapter and the challenges and opportunities for Telecom firms in the next.

But this chapter isn't a static template! The drivers for consumer demand are changing rapidly, so a good investor should regularly reassess the trends. Here, we'll review some of today's most influential developments to demonstrate how to identify new ones going forward.

EMERGING MARKETS

The industrialization and urbanization taking place in emerging markets (EMs) like China are driving enormous economic growth

Table 5.1   2009 Populations and Disposable Income (US $)

	US	Brazil	Russia	India	China
Population (MM)	307	194	141	1,166	1,335
Average Disposable Income	$32,592	$3,881	$3,970	$810	$1,134

Source: The Boston Consulting Group, "The Internet's New Billion" (September 2010).

and wealth creation. And there are still large rural populations that cell phone towers have yet to reach. Due to their growing economies and low user penetration rates, emerging markets represent a big growth opportunity for Telecom.

Disposable Income

Consumer demand for Telecom services can be heavily influenced by increases in disposable income—particularly in emerging markets. For example, someone in India with $812 of annual disposable income likely won't spend all of it on an iPhone—never mind the accompanying voice and data plan. However, India has a population of 1.17 billion, so a nominal increase in disposable income could materially impact aggregate Telecom spending in that nation. To better gauge where opportunities may be, Table 5.1 lists populations and disposable incomes for the BRIC countries (Brazil, Russia, India, and China—the largest emerging economies) and the US (for context).

Low Penetration Rates

We know India has a huge population, but investors should focus on determining the real prospect for subscriber growth. In other words, what percent of the population already pays for Telecom services (i.e., the *penetration rate*), and what percent represents an opportunity? Relative to the developed world, a number of emerging countries have low penetration rates—meaning there are still millions of potential new Telecom customers. Table 5.2 shows penetration rates for the BRIC and the US.

Table 5.2   2009 Telecom Penetration Rates for the BRIC and the US

	US	Brazil	Russia	India	China
Mobile Phone Subscriptions (MM)	279	175	197	507	769
Mobile Penetration Rate	**88%**	**86%**	**141%***	**41%**	**57%**
Internet Users (MM)	223	68	44	81	384
Internet Penetration Rate	**70%**	**33%**	**31%**	**7%**	**28%**
PCs in Use (MM)	283	66	45	55	267
PC Penetration Rate	**89%**	**32%**	**32%**	**4%**	**20%**

*Mobile phone figures were calculated using SIM (Subscriber Identity Module) card subscriptions. In Russia, there is a tendency for users to own multiple SIM cards. Therefore the actual Russian penetration rate is likely less than 100 percent.

Source: The Boston Consulting Group, "The Internet's New Billion" (September 2010).

Mobile phones have the highest penetration rates in BRIC countries compared to other technologies—not surprising considering how relatively cheap they are and the popularity of prepaid services. Prepaid services have enabled vast populations of low-income consumers to own phones because they can purchase as many minutes as they can afford. Prepaid cards can cost less than $1, and users can add value in increments as low as 30 cents.[1] In fact, it's estimated 72 percent of the world's 4.6 billion mobile subscribers use prepaid services.[2]

Although certain mobile phones can be cheap and monthly costs negligible (if the phone is used sparingly), PCs are another story. PCs can be prohibitively expensive for most BRIC citizens, and this directly impacts Internet penetration rates too, which greatly lag mobile phones' high penetration rates. However, in both India and China, Internet penetration rates are higher than PCs (see Table 5.2). In these countries (and many others), Internet cafes are still popular because they enable relatively cheap Internet use without the costs of PC ownership.

The lowest penetration rates across the board are in India. With such a large population, India is a great growth opportunity. However, the timing and pace of increased Telecom spending in India and other developing economies depends not only on the size of the population without a mobile phone, PC, or Internet connection, but on disposable income levels too.

Mobile Phone Usage

Like penetration rates, usage tends to vary by country and service. For instance, texts are wildly popular in China, but they're not half as fashionable in India. Table 5.3 lists a variety of mobile phone activities and percentage usage in the BRIC and US.

Such information can help investors identify possible opportunities. For example, a telco offering mobile gaming services in China has the potential to do well because, at a 39 percent usage rate, it's a popular activity with additional room to grow—but competition is likely high. However, using a mobile phone to make payments is less common in China than gaming—meaning there may be greater upside and less competition. Obviously, deeper research into each activity is required, but the illustration shows that user activity information can be useful in identifying consumer demand trends.

Table 5.3   2009 Percentages of Phone Users Engaging in Mobile Activities

	US	Brazil	Russia	India	China
Mobile Phone Calls	88%	99%	NA	99%	100%
Mobile Photos	60%	24%	NA	1%	49%
Mobile Internet	56%	6%	12%	1%	24%
SMS	51%	57%	80%	48%	93%
Mobile Music	36%	24%	24%	1%	47%
Mobile E-mail	21%	NA	16%	NA	20%
Ringtones	20%	NA	14%	1%	34%
Multimedia Messaging	17%	25%	36%	NA	49%
Mobile Video	16%	24%	8%	5%	26%
Mobile Gaming	12%	1%	11%	NA	39%
Mobile Payment	5%	NA	NA	NA	11%
Mobile News	2%	NA	NA	NA	23%

Source: The Boston Consulting Group, "The Internet's New Billion" (September 2010).

Wireline Usage

In general, wireline businesses are a relatively smaller portion of the emerging markets Telecom sector than wireless services (as discussed in Chapter 3). Mobile voice services are more abundant and usually more affordable than wireline voice services. However, since Internet penetration rates are relatively low in most major emerging markets, wireline businesses could benefit from greater Internet demand and therefore greater data consumption.

Similar to mobile usage, online activities vary by country too. While e-mail is common across the board, social networking is most popular in Brazil, job hunting is trendy in India, and the vast majority in China indulges in music. Depending on your outlook for these end markets, a telco delivering regionally popular services may be a relatively more attractive investment than one that doesn't. Online activities are listed by country in Table 5.4. Note the differences among the EM countries—and also between them and the US.

Table 5.4   2009 Percentages of Internet Users Engaging in Online Activities

	US	Brazil	Russia	India	China
E-mail	91%	77%	78%	95%	53%
Search Engines	89%	83%	81%	50%	69%
E-commerce	71%	17%	21%	17%	28%
Reading News	70%	47%	65%	61%	80%
Online Video	68%	49%	41%	53%	76%
Online Banking	55%	NA	11%	NA	26%
Job Hunting	51%	NA	NA	73%	19%
Instant Messaging	38%	61%	56%	62%	87%
Online Gaming	35%	44%	31%	54%	55%
Social Networking	35%	69%	15%	23%	33%
Online Music	34%	49%	47%	60%	83%
Bulletin Board/Forum	22%	18%	NA	NA	21%
Blogs	11%	17%	33%	NA	38%

Source: The Boston Consulting Group, "The Internet's New Billion" (September 2010).

DEVELOPED MARKETS

Emerging markets generally have great growth potential based on new users, but are limited by average revenue per user (ARPU) due to low incomes. The developed market is the exact opposite. Penetration rates are high, so there are limited opportunities to add subscribers, but much higher incomes support much higher ARPUs.

These demographics have coincided with two major trends in developed markets. The first is a shift from wireline to wireless services. The second is a shift from voice to data subscriptions driving growth.

Wireline to Wireless

Wireline services have been hampered by falling prices and consumers switching to wireless services. In 2006 dollars, US Telecom firms' wireline revenue per minute peaked at $4.27 in 1933 and has dropped to $0.07 in 2006—the 73-year decline is shown in Figure 5.1. As prices

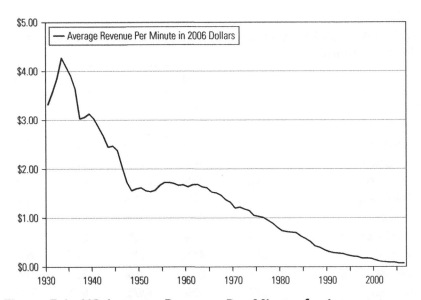

Figure 5.1   US Average Revenue Per Minute for Interstate and International Calls

Source: Federal Communications Commission, "Trends in Telephone Service: 1930–2006" (August 2008), p.104.

fell, consumers used more minutes, but even falling costs have done little to stem the tide of decreased wireline spending in US households. As shown in Figure 5.2, household wireline spending peaked in 1997 at $57 per month and has declined ever since.

Wireless household spending stands in stark contrast to the decline in wireline spending. As shown in Figure 5.2, the growth in wireless spending has been strong enough to more than offset the decline in wireline spending and has powered aggregate Telecom spending higher.

In the mid-1990s, the initial rise in wireless spending was driven by early cell phone adopters—those willing to pay a premium for a service not yet widespread. However, as the mobile industry matured, the quality and affordability of wireless services led to more consumers not only buying cell phones, but also canceling their traditional wireline services.

Figure 5.2 provides an excellent look at household Telecom spending, but it's also important to consider business spending. Unlike a

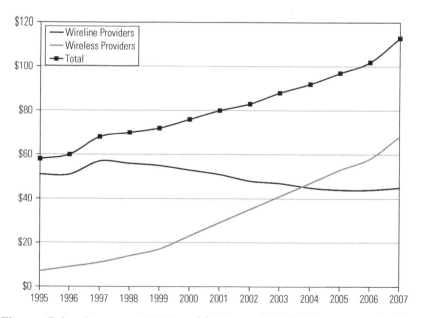

Figure 5.2   Average US Monthly Household Telecommunication Expenditures

Source: Federal Communications Commission, "Trends in Telephone Service: 1995–2007" (August 2008), p. 29.

home, it's unlikely a business will cancel all wireline phones and just use cell phones. But even accounting for both homes and businesses, mobile revenue growth has still been astounding. In 1997, mobile accounted for just 22 percent of all OECD Telecom revenue—by 2007, it was 41 percent (the OECD is mainly developed countries, so it's a fine proxy for the developed world even though it does contain some small non-BRIC EM countries). It's likely this trend will continue, especially due to the growing popularity of smartphones.

Smartphones The migration from wireline to wireless has been expedited by the popularity of smartphones, whose demand is growing six times faster than the overall mobile phone market.[3] Whereas smartphones were an insignificant percent of wireless market share just a few years ago, in 2009, nearly 32 percent of AT&T's postpaid (customers on contracts) mobile subscribers were using a smartphone.[4] The growth has been fast—particularly for AT&T because of the popularity of the Apple iPhone. (AT&T had an edge in attracting new subscribers because it was the sole US provider of the iPhone when the phone launched in 2007. As of February 2011, however, AT&T lost exclusivity, and Verizon also began offering the iPhone.)

Figure 5.3 shows the growth of mobile subscribers in OECD countries. Because the figure shows growth only through 2007, it doesn't reflect the more recent growth of the smartphone market, but it's interesting to note the increasing popularity of prepaid phones. The economical attributes that make prepaid phones popular in emerging markets are attractive in developed countries too—segments like the youth market, families, and small business customers (who prefer to control usage or pay in advance) also favor prepaid subscriptions.

Voice to Data

As the price and importance of voice services have fallen for both wireline and wireless services, data services have filled the void and

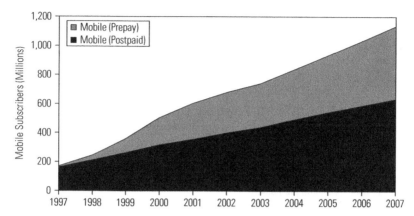

Figure 5.3   Cellular Mobile Subscribers in OECD Countries

Source: Organisation for Economic Co-operation and Development, "OECD Communications Outlook 2009."

fueled growth. Data demand has been driven in wireline by broadband demand and in wireless by smartphones.

Although broadband prices have been falling—between 2005 and 2008, Digital Subscriber Line (DSL) prices fell in the OECD by 14 percent per year[5]—subscription growth has coincided with greater data demand. Due to consumers' desire to participate in the numerous activities listed in Table 5.4, broadband has grown from 60 percent of OECD wireline Internet connections in 2005 to 90 percent in 2007.[6]

Web browsing, e-mailing, GPS maps, social networking, and the thousands of applications that can now be run on a smartphone have driven considerably more demand for mobile data. The significance of the growth can be exemplified by AT&T. Between 2006 and 2009, AT&T's annual wireless data revenue grew 47 percent annually to $14.3 billion. Wireless data skyrocketed from only 4.6 percent of company revenue in 2006 to 11.5 percent in 2009. Smartphones have contributed to the growth of wireless not only through handset sales, but by driving increased demand for mobile data, which bolsters ARPUs.

Chapter Recap

The Telecom sector has undergone significant changes because of deregulation and new technologies. In order to increase the likelihood of identifying the investment opportunities that are created by change, it's important to understand what's driving consumer demand for Telecom services. Here are some of the most influential trends today:

- In numerous EMs, there are growth opportunities based on large populations with low penetration rates. Disposable incomes, however, are often low, which limits Telecom spending per person.

- In EMs, mobile and wireline usage differs regionally.

- In developed markets, there are few opportunities to add subscribers, but higher disposable income drives higher ARPUs.

- There have been two primary trends in developed markets: A transition from wireline to wireless services, and a shift from voice to data subscriptions driving growth.

6

CHALLENGES AND OPPORTUNITIES

Understanding the unique challenges a sector faces can help investors better shape forward-looking expectations for the sector. Challenges aren't always all negative—they can also frequently morph into opportunities for the firms and industries that can rise above. This chapter will detail some of the major challenges and opportunities Telecom firms face by examining AT&T's revenues. AT&T is a decent proxy for the sector overall and is useful for this particular exercise because its diverse business segments encompass the same businesses as the vast majority of other Telecom firms. *This should NOT be taken as an endorsement for or against AT&T.*

A great place to start gathering information about AT&T, or any publicly traded firm, is its *annual report*, which can be found on the firm's website or its EDGAR filings at www.sec.gov. Such filings include earnings, profit margins, and a whole slew of information further detailed in Chapter 8. But for our current purposes, we'll take a look at AT&T's 2009 sales in Table 6.1. Also, we'll focus more on Wireline and Wireless than Advertising & Publishing because they represent greater percentages of total revenue and therefore likely play a larger

Table 6.1   AT&T's 2009 Revenues

Business Segment	Percent of Company Revenue
Wireline	**53%**
Voice	27%
Data	21%
Other	5%
Wireless	**43%**
Voice	28%
Data	11%
Equipment	4%
Advertising & Publishing	**4%**

Source: AT&T 2009 Form 10-K.

role in determining AT&T's performance in the near term (12 to 24 months).

WIRELINE

Wireline is the vast network of wires and computers (switches) that are the infrastructure for the Internet and local and long-distance calls. Despite the prevalence of cell phones and new technologies, wireline remains 53 percent of AT&T's revenue—a significant portion and therefore an important business to understand. Wireline is composed of three segments:

1. Voice (27 percent of firm revenue) includes traditional local and long-distance service provided to retail customers and wholesale access to its network.
2. Data (21 percent of firm revenue) is the high-growth segment of AT&T's wireline business and includes traditional products, such as switched and dedicated transport, Internet access and network integration, data equipment sales, U-verse (AT&T's cable television service), and Voice over Internet Protocol (VoIP).

3. Other (5 percent of firm revenue) is composed of an assortment of services, like security and disaster recovery services. Since it's a relatively small portion of the company's top line, it will likely be marginally important.

Challenges

The primary challenge for wireline is the demise of the Voice segment—it's a mature business with intense competition. Deregulation increased the number of local and long distance providers, and technology has shepherded in new competitors like cable and VoIP. Furthermore, as detailed in Chapter 4, there are usually numerous political risks (like net neutrality—the regulatory challenge du jour).

Cable   Cable firms now contend for the same residential wireline customers as telcos. Cable firms have made big investments in equipment and facilities to provide more than just TV signals. Their special coaxial cable wires can handle large amounts of data to transmit VoIP telephone calls, Internet access, hundreds of TV channels, HDTV, on-demand programs, etc. As cable offerings further saturate US households, cable firms take phone and broadband market share at the expense of wireline providers like AT&T. And the trend is likely to continue.

In fact, cable appears likely to go after what remains—wireless. Some US cable companies are now creating free Wi-Fi hotspots to improve customer retention rates—likely part of a larger wireless strategy. The difference between cable and telecom companies will likely become smaller and smaller. They may someday even be classified in the same investment sector!

A big reason for cable firms' success in taking market share is their ability to capitalize on low-cost VoIP services, which are popular with consumers because they're usually "all you can eat" at a fixed price.

Voice Over Internet Protocol (VoIP)   VoIP, a recent technological innovation, is an alternative to traditional voice services. VoIP converts an analog signal (in this case, the human voice) into digitized units that are bundled into packets and sent over the Internet. At the receiving end, the packets are reassembled into an analog voice signal and voilà—a phone conversation not subject to the static and faintness of all-copper networks. And it's cheap because the cost is largely equal to the minuscule amount of Internet bandwidth used.

Because VoIP uses existing Internet infrastructure, huge network expenditures aren't necessary. The resulting low barrier to entry has given rise to numerous VoIP providers (such as Skype and Vonage and there are dozens more in the US alone). VoIP is not only a US or residential market phenomenon—it's global and especially popular with business customers. To compete, AT&T and other telcos now offer their own VoIP services. However, even if they manage to retain VoIP customers, it often cannibalizes Voice revenue—a choice they must make.

Although VoIP's threat is considerable, it was previously even greater. Prior to 2006, it had additional cost advantages in the US because it was not required to make contributions to the Universal Service Fund and pay termination charges like its beleaguered Voice peers.

Net Neutrality   By levying VoIP providers the same taxes as traditional Voice, regulators helped to level the competitive playing field somewhat. But with *net neutrality*, regulators could completely reconfigure the field.

Net neutrality is sought by the FCC to regulate how phone and cable companies handle web traffic. On one hand, net neutrality proponents believe restrictions are required so firms providing Internet services do not favor their own online offerings or those of partners that pay a premium for higher speeds. The concern is service providers will use tiered services to create artificial scarcity and remove competition.

On the other hand, telcos believe net neutrality will force them to be "dumb pipes"—nothing more than utilities providing pipes of Internet bandwidth at regulated prices. Telcos, like AT&T, believe they should have opportunities to be compensated for the financial risks of building a network—otherwise, why be in business?

Moreover, they claim data discrimination is required at some level to guarantee quality of service for all users.

As of this book's writing, it appears net neutrality is unlikely to pass—the Republicans have gained a majority in the House, and major broadband consumers like Google have made usage agreements with service providers like Verizon instead of waiting for regulators to come up with their own rules.

Nevertheless, even if the likelihood of net neutrality passing is currently low, it poses a considerable challenge because it's difficult to predict the unintended consequences of regulation. Try as they might, legislators have shown a great propensity to not understand the domino effect of interjecting themselves into free markets. Not all regulation is bad, of course, and historically, increased regulation has often benefited telcos—but frequently to the detriment of consumers. Even the most well-intended regulatory changes can have deleterious side effects that are difficult, if not impossible, to predict.

Opportunities

Because Voice is challenged by intense competition and Data may be significantly impacted by regulation, firms reliant on those business lines (like AT&T) must look for opportunities to offset or overcome challenges. Some opportunities are obvious—for example, AT&T, like many Baby Bells searching for additional revenue and earnings, leases network services and capacity to competitors, which contributes considerably to its Voice revenue.

Nevertheless, the wireline business remains difficult. For decades, traditional Voice has been the cash cow, but revenues have been declining and that will likely continue. In order to address the numerous challenges and consumer demand trends listed in Chapter 5, the sections in this chapter will outline some initiatives wireline businesses have undertaken.

Fiber-Optic Cable   Copper, still used in many local telecom connections, has increasingly been replaced by fiber optic cable, which is capable of transmitting much more data. In the US, AT&T and

Fiber-Optic Cables

A fiber-optic cable is 1/25th the width of a human hair and carries light pulses that are converted into digital ones and zeros—binary digits called bits. In order to maximize how many bits can be sent over a network, numerous fiber-optic cables are bundled together. Although a fiber-optic cable is usually made of silica, the most common mineral in the earth's crust and a fraction of the cost of an equivalent length of copper wire, the equipment costs to transmit the data are much greater—and therefore the costs to upgrade to fiber optics can be substantial.

Verizon have been extending fiber-optic cables to neighborhoods and homes, providing Internet access with speeds up to 20 times faster than traditional broadband.[1] Greater capacity has provided the opportunity for Telecom firms to compete more aggressively with the high bandwidth delivered by cable companies and offer the same TV channels, HDTV, and video on demand.

Bundling   Initially, firms like AT&T entered the wireless market to position themselves for growth and to offset a declining wireline business. As both wireline and wireless markets have matured, however, new products and services have been sought to fuel growth and improve customer retention rates.

Now that fiber-optic cables have enabled telephone firms to offer video, they can bundle services. Consumers like bundling because it can be more convenient (one bill) and typically provides greater savings and utility. And firms like it because it can improve client retention. Furthermore, by selling customers more services, the ARPU often increases, even if the price for each individual service is discounted.

The "triple play" (voice, video, and data services) originated with cable providers and was quickly matched by Telecom firms. However, due to the limitations of copper wires at the time, video was initially provided to Telecom customers through partnerships with satellite service providers. Recently, Telecom firms caught up to cable companies by offering their own fiber optic–based video—and have surpassed them (for now) by adding wireless services to the bundle and making it a "quadruple play."

Time to Market   In the not-so-distant future, there will likely be a race to offer a "quintuple play"—whatever that fifth service may be. By being first to market, a service provider has the opportunity to woo customers from competitors. But while this can be a powerful opportunity, the competition will eventually catch up, the benefit of the lead will diminish, and the race will be for the "sextuple play."

Consolidation   When competitors catch up to each other and services become more commoditized, profit margins shrink. As a result, wireline businesses have sought to either diversify into higher growth products like television and VoIP—or to consolidate.

In a mature and competitive market like wireline, consolidation can be an opportunity to increase revenue and earnings. Often, just being bigger is better. Greater operating leverage and economies of scale can provide slightly better margins that make one company a more attractive investment than another. The opportunity for consolidation is well exemplified by Frontier Communications—a rural service provider.

Consolidation has been a strong force for rural service providers, whose costs can be especially high because of low population densities and are therefore subsidized by the Universal Service Fund. Frontier Communications bought numerous rural networks from competitors seeking to get out of the low-margin rural regions—in 2010, it paid Verizon $8.6 billion to acquire 4.8 million landlines. Such acquisitions represent opportunities for buyers to improve operating leverage and for sellers to get out of businesses that can be relatively unattractive.

WIRELESS

Wireless communications require radio frequencies (rather than a wire) to carry a signal over part of or the entire communication path. AT&T's wireless business has grown significantly and now accounts for 43 percent of the company's total revenue (see Table 6.1). Wireless is composed of three segments:

1. Voice (28 percent of company revenue) includes postpaid customers (users with one- or two-year contracts) and prepaid customers (usually the youth market, families, and small business customers who prefer to control usage or pay in advance).
2. Data (11 percent of company revenue) is the higher-growth segment of AT&T's wireless business. It includes both consumer and enterprise wireless data services for handsets and more advanced integrated devices like e-readers and notebooks.
3. Equipment (4 percent of company revenue) includes handsets, wireless-enabled computers (i.e., notebooks and netbooks), and personal computer wireless data cards manufactured by various suppliers for use with voice and data services. As a relatively small portion of the company's top line, it will likely play a marginal role in determining AT&T's performance in the near term.

Challenges

Due to its relatively low penetration rates in emerging markets and higher ARPU in developed markets (because of data plans), wireless is generally the growth business for Telecom firms—but competition is fierce and businesses face numerous challenges.

Little Differentiation   Ideally, AT&T could easily and convincingly differentiate its services from competitors like Verizon. But the reality is wireless services are just slightly less commoditized than wireline services—one company's wireless minutes are no different from another's, driving down prices and resulting in a decline in wireless voice ARPU. Moreover, services like call waiting and caller ID, which were additional fees, are now free. Even unlimited voice and unlimited texts are now standard (for a price).

Network quality (dropped calls) and coverage area can be differentiators for wireless providers, but they're often not convincing enough in many areas to drive a consumer's carrier decision.

Low Switching Costs   When there is little differentiation between wireless offerings, there are low switching costs. If an AT&T customer lives in a region where Verizon's network quality and coverage area are similar, he has little reason to stay loyal to AT&T—he can switch when Verizon offers a superior deal. Low switching costs result in high churn rates (attrition), which is bad for any business.

Prepaid   AT&T's wireless business not only competes with the other three major service providers (Verizon, Sprint, and T-Mobile) in the postpaid US market, but competes with them in the prepaid market too. The prepaid market (consumers are not on contract; they prepay for minutes) is defined by aggressive price competition among the big four and a slew of prepaid-only providers, like TracFone (owned by America Movil).

Postpaid customers usually generate higher ARPUs than prepaid ones, so any gain in prepaid's wireless market share is a threat to company revenue and earnings. And as you can imagine, prepaid's market share typically rises during recessions since consumers usually have less to spend and credit requirements for postpaid plans are more stringent.

Opportunities

To combat fierce competition and wireless challenges, wireless businesses like AT&T's are constantly seeking opportunities to better retain and grow their number of wireless subscribers, revenue, and earnings.

Data   Data has been the most significant opportunity for wireless providers to offset the decline in wireless voice ARPU. Smartphones have been a savior—as consumers and businesses upgrade their handsets to more integrated devices, like Apple's iPhone or RIM's BlackBerries, data plans are often purchased for amounts equal to or greater than the voice service. In addition to data plan revenue, there are opportunities to sell a wide range of other services to handsets boasting a host of other features, like music downloads, games, video on demand, mobile applications, mobile banking, etc.

The rise in wireless data consumption is also aided by the rapid growth in demand for new wireless devices like laptops, Amazon's Kindle, and Apple's iPad. However, the spike in wireless data demand has put increasing burdens on networks.

Next Generation Networks   Carriers may choose to invest heavily to upgrade their networks, expand capacity, and offer better call quality and data speeds than their competitors—a company can choose to simply expand the current network capacity or upgrade to the next generation of wireless technology. In both cases, the opportunity is to improve wireless subscription numbers and to have the capacity to sell more data-intensive services.

Handsets   Carriers have sought to motivate customers to upgrade from low-end phones to smartphones—they are a primary driver for

Wireless Technologies

There are numerous technical buzzwords in the wireless industry—here are a couple of the most common:

- GSM and CDMA: These are the two leading standards for mobile telephony systems. Global System for Mobile Communications (GSM) is the most popular in the world, is used by AT&T and T-Mobile in the US, and is common in Europe. Code Division Multiple Access (CDMA) is the standard used by Sprint and Verizon in the US, and in parts of Asia.

- 1G/2G/3G/4G: Each "G" corresponds to a generation of cellular wireless standards and increasing data capacities. 1G is an analog transmission, 2G is a digital transmission, 3G is a spread spectrum transmission, and 4G is an all Internet Protocol packet-switched network. In many developed countries, where data demand is high, 4G networks are being built using one of two competing technologies: Long Term Evolution (LTE) and WiMAX.

wireless data consumption and revenue. One of the most successful strategies to attract upgrades and new clients is exclusivity on a
"must-have" phone, as AT&T did with Apple's iPhone. Although
it's not known how much AT&T paid for years of exclusivity, it was
likely worthwhile because consumers flocked to AT&T, locked themselves into minimum two-year contracts, and also upgraded to its data
plans. Because wireless services are pretty fungible, handset exclusivity
can be a big opportunity for a carrier to stand out from the crowd.

Pricing   Opportunities to improve client retention rates and ARPU
often involve pricing strategies. A common tactic is to subsidize a
consumer's handset price for a two-year contract. For example, both
Verizon and AT&T sell a $599 16GB Apple iPhone 4 for $199 with a
two-year contract. The price attracts consumers who cannot pay $599
up front or those looking for a deal. The carriers more than make up
for the cost of the subsidy with the phone's accompanying data
plan—plus the contract ensures a more predictable and stable revenue
stream.

Even if a carrier does not have an "it" phone, there are opportunities to market phones and data plans to a wide range of consumer segments. For example, instead of one "all-you-can-eat" data plan, which
is too expensive for many consumers, wireless providers have recently
rolled out tiered pricing plans for a wider range of data consumption.

Family Plans   Family plans are another opportunity to increase
retention rates and revenue and cash flow predictability. Family plans
allow additional cell phone users to be added to a plan for as little as
$10 per month. The low costs reduce ARPU, but similar to the bun-
dling strategy mentioned previously, by simplifying billing and offering greater value, it is less likely a customer will switch to a competing
carrier.

Spectrum   The opportunity to own spectrum is valuable because it's
a finite resource and is needed to offer wireless services. In the US,
for example, AT&T and Verizon have a material advantage over their

competitors because their spectrum portfolios are much more extensive. Carriers with less spectrum may not be able to offer comparable data speeds and will likely need to spend more on building cell sites to more efficiently use the spectrum they do have. Often, the larger wireless companies have an advantage in acquiring spectrum because they are more able to afford the large sums governments charge.

Innovation   Rapid innovation has created numerous wireless opportunities in a short period. Such change and opportunity can be exemplified by Apple's iPhone, which sold millions of handsets in just a few years, spawned the development of thousands of applications, and expedited consumer demand for wireless data plans.

Companies can successfully innovate beyond just product and service offerings. Bharti Airtel, India's largest wireless provider, has grown rapidly by adopting an innovative business model. It's practically a virtual business—its network is supplied by Ericsson, and its IT and billing are handled by IBM—it manages only sales and marketing!

ADVERTISING & PUBLISHING

Advertising & Publishing (only 4 percent of AT&T's revenue) produces the Yellow and White Pages directories and sells directory advertising, Internet-based advertising, and local search. Although it's a small portion of AT&T's revenue and therefore an unlikely determinant of operating results in the near term, Advertising & Publishing has been surprising resilient—Yellow Pages ad revenue is $13 billion per year in the US, which is more than all magazine advertising combined.[2]

The challenges for published directories include high competition (there are more than 200 Yellow Pages publishers in the US[3]), the public's growing use of Internet services, and diminishing use of paper directories. Additionally, there are some state legislative initiatives to get rid of the Yellow Pages because they annually account for more than five pounds of paper for each man, woman, and child in the US.[4] White Pages are not threatened because they are required by law in most states, but they generate little to no ad revenue for publishers.

In the long run, the opportunities in Advertising & Publishing appear to lie in Internet-based ads—it seems likely the industry will eventually need to consolidate to maintain competitiveness in the face of declining use.

Chapter Summary

By marrying the trends in consumer demand from the last chapter and the challenges and opportunities from this chapter, an investor should be able to hypothesize which Telecom industries and companies should benefit from prevailing trends. Here are some of the major threats and opportunities:

- The primary challenge for wireline businesses is the demise of the voice segment—it's a mature business with intense competition. Moreover, the data segment is threatened not only by competition, but by possible regulation too.

- The opportunities for Wireline lie in its ability to increase data speeds and offer more services. Also, it can improve operating performance through consolidation and can increase subscriber retention rates by bundling services.

- Wireless's challenges are similar to Wireline's. There's little differentiation in services and switching costs are low, which result in a competitive environment.

- Wireless's opportunities are to increase services and products that drive data demand, which has been a primary growth driver. Handset pricing and family plans are strategies to increase subscriber retention rates.

III

THINKING LIKE A PORTFOLIO MANAGER

7

THE TOP-DOWN METHOD

If you're bullish on Telecommunications, how much of your portfolio should you put in Telecommunications stocks? Twenty-five percent? Fifty? One hundred percent? This question concerns portfolio management. Most investors concern themselves only with individual companies ("I like AT&T, so I'll buy some") without considering how they fit into their overall portfolio. But this is no way to manage your money.

In Part III of this book, we show you how to analyze Telecommunications companies like a top-down portfolio manager. This includes a full description of the top-down method, how to use benchmarks, and how the top-down method applies to the Telecommunications sector. We then explore security analysis in Chapter 8, where we provide a framework for analyzing any company and discuss many of the important questions to ask when analyzing Telecommunications companies. Finally, in Chapter 9, we conclude by giving a few examples of specific investing strategies for the Telecommunications sector.

INVESTING IS A SCIENCE

Too many investors today think investing has "rules"—that all one must do to succeed in investing for the long run is find the right set of investing rules. But that simply doesn't work. Why? All well-known and widely discussed information is already reflected in stock prices. This is a basic tenet of market theory and commonly referred to as "market efficiency." So if you see a headline about a stock you follow, there's no use trading on that information—it's already priced in. You missed the move.

If everything known is already discounted in prices, the only way to consistently beat the market is to know something others don't. Think about it: There are many intelligent investors and longtime professionals who fail to beat the market year after year, most with the same access to information as anyone, if not more. Why?

Most view investing as a craft. They think, "If I learn the craft of value investing and all its rules, then I can be a successful investor using that method." But that simply can't work because by definition, all the conventional ways of thinking about value investing will already be widely known and thus priced in. In fact, most investment styles are well-known and already widely practiced. There are undoubtedly millions of investors out there much like you, looking at the same metrics and information you are. So there isn't much power in them. Even the investing techniques themselves are widely known—taught to millions in universities and practiced by hundreds of thousands of professionals globally. There's no edge.

Moreover, it's been demonstrated that investment styles move in and out of favor over time—no one style or category is inherently better than another in the long run. You may think "value" investing works wonders to beat markets, but the fact is growth stocks will trounce value at times.

The key to beating stock markets lies in being dynamic—never adhering for all time to a single investment idea—and gleaning information the market hasn't yet priced in. In other words, you cannot stick to a single set of "rules" and hope to outperform markets over time.

So how can you beat the markets? By thinking of investing as a science.

EINSTEIN'S BRAIN AND THE STOCK MARKET

If he hadn't been so busy becoming the most renowned scientist of the twentieth century, Albert Einstein would have made a killing on Wall Street—but not because he had such a high IQ. Granted, he was immensely intelligent, but a high IQ alone does not make a market guru. (If it did, MIT professors would be making millions managing money instead of teaching.) Instead, it's the style of his thought and the method of his work that matter.

From the little we know about Einstein's investment track record, he didn't do well. He lost most of his Nobel Prize money in bad bond ventures.[1] Heck, Sir Isaac Newton may have given us the three laws of motion, but even his talents didn't extend to investing. He lost his shirt in the South Sea Bubble of the early 1700s, explaining later, "I can calculate the movement of the stars, but not the madness of men."

So why believe Einstein would have been a great portfolio manager if he put his mind to it? In short, Einstein was a true and highly creative scientist. He didn't take the acknowledged rules of physics as such—he used prior knowledge, logic, and creativity combined with the rigors of verifiable, testable scientific method to create an entirely new view of the cosmos. In other words, he was dynamic and gleaned knowledge others didn't have. Investors should do the same. (Not to worry, you won't need advanced calculus to do it.)

Einstein's unique character gave him an edge—he truly had a mind made to beat markets. Scientists have studied his work, his speeches, his letters, even his brain (literally) to find the secret of his intellect. In all, his approach to information processing and idea generation, his willingness to go against the grain of the establishment, and his relentless pursuit of answers to questions no one else was asking ultimately made him a genius.

Most biographers and his contemporaries agree one of Einstein's foremost gifts was his ability to discern "the big picture." Unlike many scientists who could easily drown themselves in data minutiae, Einstein had an ability to see above the fray. Another way to say this is he could take the same information everyone else in his time was looking at and interpret it differently, yet correctly. He accomplished this using his talent for extracting the most important data from what he studied and linking them together in innovative ways no one else could.

Einstein called this "combinatory play." Similar to a child experimenting with a new Lego set, Einstein would combine and recombine seemingly unrelated ideas, concepts, and images to produce new, original discoveries. In the end, most all new ideas are merely the combination of existing ones in one form or another. Take $E = mc^2$: Einstein was not the first to discover the concepts of energy, mass, or the speed of light; rather, he combined these concepts in a novel way, and in the process, altered the way in which we view the universe.[2]

Einstein's combinatory play is a terrific metaphor for stock investing. To be a successful market strategist, you must be able to extract the most important data from all of the "noise" permeating today's markets and generate conclusions the market hasn't yet appreciated. Central to this task is your ability to link data together in unique ways and produce new insights and themes for your portfolio in the process.

Einstein learned science basics just like his peers. But after he had those mastered, he directed his brain to challenging prior assumptions and inventing entirely different lenses to look through.

This is why this book isn't intended to give you a "silver bullet" for picking the right Telecommunications stocks. The fact is the "right" Telecommunications stocks will be different in different times and situations. You don't have to be like an Einstein, you should just think differently—and like a scientist—if you want to beat markets.

THE TOP-DOWN METHOD

Overwhelmingly, investment professionals today do what can be broadly labeled "bottom-up" investing. Their emphasis is on stock selection. A typical bottom-up investor researches an assortment of companies and attempts to pick those with the greatest likelihood of outperforming the market based on individual merits. The selected securities are cobbled together to form a portfolio, and factors like country and economic sector exposure are purely residuals of security selection, not planned decisions.

"Top-down" investing reverses the order. A top-down investor first analyzes big picture factors like economics, politics, and sentiment to forecast which investment categories are most likely to outperform the market. Only then does a top-down investor begin looking at individual securities. Top-down investing is inevitably more concerned with a portfolio's aggregate exposure to investment categories than with any individual security. Thus, top-down is an inherently dynamic mode of investing because investment strategies are based upon the prevailing market and economic environments (which change often).

There's significant debate in the investment community as to which approach is superior. This book's goal is not to reject bottom-up investing—there are indeed investors who've successfully utilized bottom-up approaches. Rather, the goal is to introduce a comprehensive and flexible methodology any investor could use to build a portfolio designed to beat the global stock market in any investment environment. It's a framework for gleaning new insights and making good on information not already reflected in stock prices.

Before we describe the method, let's explore several key reasons a top-down approach is advantageous:

- **Scalability.** A bottom-up process is akin to looking for needles in a haystack. A top-down process is akin to seeking the haystacks with the highest concentrations of needles. Globally, there are nearly 25,000 publicly traded stocks. Even the largest institutions with the greatest research resources cannot hope to adequately examine all these companies. Smaller institutions and individual investors must prioritize where to focus their limited resources. Unlike a bottom-up process, a top-down process makes this gargantuan task manageable by determining upfront what slices of the market to examine at the security level.
- **Enhanced stock selection.** Well-designed top-down processes generate insights that can greatly enhance stock selection. Macroeconomic or political analysis, for instance, can help

determine what types of strategic attributes will face head- or tailwinds (see Chapter 8 for a full explanation).

- **Risk control.** Bottom-up processes are highly subject to unintended risk concentrations. Top-down processes are inherently better suited to manage risk exposures throughout the investment process.
- **Macro overview.** Top-down processes are more conducive to avoiding macro-driven calamities like the bursting of the Japan bubble in the 1990s, the Technology bubble in 2000, or the bear market of 2000 to 2002. No matter how good an individual company may be, it is still beholden to sector, regional, and broad market factors. In fact, there is evidence "macro" factors can largely determine a stock's performance regardless of individual merit.

Top-Down Means Thinking 70-20-10

A top-down investment process also helps focus on what's most important to investment results: asset allocation and sub-asset allocation decisions. Many investors focus most of their attention on security-level portfolio decisions, like picking individual stocks they think will perform well. However, studies have shown that over 90 percent of return variability is derived from asset allocation decisions, not market timing or stock selection.[3]

Our research shows about 70 percent of return variability is derived from asset allocation, 20 percent from sub-asset allocation (such as country, sector, size, and style), and 10 percent from security selection. Although security selection can make a significant difference over time, higher-level portfolio decisions dominate investment results more often than not.

The balance of this chapter defines the various steps in the top-down method, specifically as they relate to making country, sector, and style decisions. This same basic framework can be applied to portfolios to make allocations within sectors. At the end of the chapter, we detail how this framework can be applied to the Telecommunications sector.

Benchmarks

A key part of the top-down model is using benchmarks. A *benchmark* is typically a broad-based index of securities such as the S&P 500, MSCI World, or Russell 2000. Benchmarks are indispensible road-maps for structuring a portfolio, monitoring risk, and judging performance over time.

Tactically, a portfolio should be structured to maximize the probability of consistently beating the benchmark. This is inherently different from maximizing returns. Unlike aiming to achieve some fixed rate of return each year, which will cause disappointment relative to peers when capital markets are strong and is potentially unrealistic when the capital markets are weak, a properly benchmarked portfolio provides a realistic guide for dealing with uncertain market conditions.

Portfolio construction begins by evaluating the characteristics of the chosen benchmark: sector weights, country weights, and market cap and valuations. Then an expected risk and return is assigned to each of these segments (based on portfolio drivers), and the most attractive areas are overweighted, while the least attractive are underweighted. Table 7.1 shows MSCI World benchmark sector characteristics

Table 7.1   MSCI World Characteristics—Sectors

Sector	Total
Financials	20.4%
Information Technology	12.0%
Industrials	11.0%
Consumer Staples	10.5%
Health Care	10.2%
Energy	9.9%
Consumer Discretionary	9.9%
Materials	7.3%
Utilities	4.4%
Telecommunication Services	4.2%

Note: Sector weights do not sum to 100% due to rounding.
Source: Thomson Reuters; MSCI, Inc.[4] MSCI World Index as of 12/31/09.

Table 7.2   MSCI World Characteristics—Countries

Country	Total
USA	49.6%
Japan	10.4%
United Kingdom	9.5%
Canada	5.2%
France	4.4%
Australia	3.7%
Switzerland	3.6%
Germany	3.5%
Spain	1.6%
Sweden	1.3%
Italy	1.3%
Netherlands	1.2%
Hong Kong	1.1%
Singapore	0.8%
Finland	0.5%
Denmark	0.5%
Belgium	0.4%
Israel	0.4%
Norway	0.3%
Austria	0.1%
Ireland	0.1%
Greece	0.1%
Portugal	0.1%
New Zealand	0.0%

Note: Country weights do not sum to 100% due to rounding.
Source: Thomson Reuters; MSCI, Inc.,[5] MSCI World Index as of 12/31/09.

as of December 31, 2009 as an example. Table 7.2 shows country characteristics, and Table 7.3 shows market cap and valuations.

Based on benchmark characteristics, portfolio drivers are then used to determine country, sector, and style decisions for the portfolio. For example, the Financials sector weight in the MSCI World Index is about 20 percent. Therefore, a portfolio managed against this benchmark would consider a 20 percent weight in Financials "neutral," or

Table 7.3 MSCI World Characteristics—Market Cap and Valuations

	Valuations
Weighted Average Market Cap	61,004
Median Market Cap	6,827
Median P/E	16.1
Median P/B	1.8
Median P/CF	10.3
Median P/S	1.4
Median Dividend Yield	1.8
Number of Holdings	1,656

Notes: Market Cap in US Billions, P/E = price to earnings, P/B = price to book, P/CF = price to cash flow, P/S = price to sales.
Source: Thomson Reuters; MSCI, Inc.,[6] MSCI World Index as of 12/31/09.

market-weighted. If you believe Financials will perform better than the market in the foreseeable future, then you would "overweight" the sector, or carry a percentage of stocks in your portfolio greater than 20 percent. The reverse is true for an "underweight"—you'd hold less than 20 percent in Financials if you were pessimistic about the sector looking ahead.

Note that being pessimistic about Financials doesn't necessarily mean holding zero stocks. It might only mean holding a lesser percentage of stocks in your portfolio than the benchmark. This is an important feature of benchmarking—it allows an investor to make strategic decisions on sectors and countries but maintains diversification, thus managing risk appropriately.

For the Telecommunications sector, we can use Telecommunications-specific benchmarks like the S&P 500 Telecommunications, MSCI World Telecommunications, or Russell 2000 Telecommunications indexes. The components of these benchmarks can then be evaluated at a more detailed level such as industry and sub-industry weights. (For example, we broke out MSCI World industry and sub-industry benchmark weights in Chapter 3.)

TOP-DOWN DECONSTRUCTED

The top-down method begins by first analyzing the macro environment. It asks the "big" questions like: Do you think stocks will go up or down in the next 12 months? If so, which countries or sectors should benefit most? Once you have decided on these high-level portfolio "drivers" (sometimes called "themes"), you can examine various macro portfolio drivers to make general overweight and underweight decisions for countries, sectors, industries, and sub-industries versus your benchmark.

For instance, let's say we've determined a macroeconomic driver that goes something like this: "In the next 12 months, I believe global economic growth will be slower than most expect." That's a high-level statement with important implications for your portfolio. It means you'd want to search for stocks that would benefit most from weakening economic growth and activity.

The second step in top-down is applying quantitative screening criteria to narrow the choice set of stocks. Since we believe economic growth will be weak in our hypothetical example, it likely means we're bullish on Telecom stocks, given the sector's defensive nature.

But which ones? Are you bullish on, say, Integrated? Wireless? Alternative Carriers? Do you want exposure to the US or another region? Do you want small cap Telecommunications companies or large cap? And what about valuations? Are you looking for growth or value? (Size and growth/value categories are often referred to as "style" decisions.) These criteria and more can help you narrow the list of stocks you might buy.

The third and final step is performing fundamental analysis on individual stocks. Notice a great deal of thinking, analysis, and work is done before you ever consider individual stocks. That's the key to the top-down approach: It emphasizes high-level themes and funnels its way down to individual stocks, as illustrated in Figure 7.1.

Step 1: Analyze Portfolio Drivers and Country and Sector Selection

Let's examine the first step in the top-down method more closely. In order to make top-down decisions, we develop and analyze what

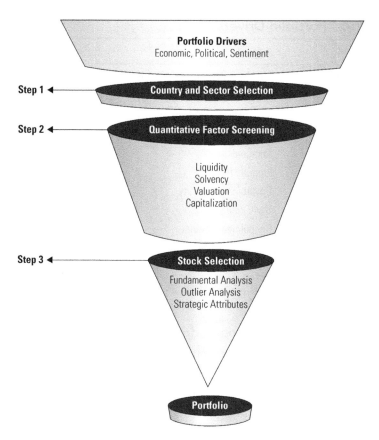

Figure 7.1   Top-Down Deconstructed

we call *portfolio drivers* (as mentioned previously). We segment these portfolio drivers in three general categories: economic, political, and sentiment.

Portfolio drivers are what drive performance of a broad category of stocks. Accurately identifying current and future drivers will help you find areas of the market most likely to outperform or underperform your benchmark (i.e., the broader stock market).

Table 7.4 shows examples of each type of portfolio driver. It's important to note these drivers are by no means comprehensive, nor are they valid for all time periods. In fact, correctly identifying new portfolio drivers is essential to beating the market in the long term.

Table 7.4   Portfolio Drivers

Economic	Political	Sentiment
Economic Growth	Structural Reform/Liberalization	Growth vs. Value
Interest Rates	Energy & Environmental Policy	Mutual Fund Flows
Inflation	Nationalization/Privatization	Media Coverage
Commodity Prices	Regulatory Environment	Consumer Confidence
Capital Investment	Taxation	Risk Aversion
Industrial Production	Property Rights	Large vs. Small Cap
Employment	Government Stability	Foreign Investment
Housing Markets	Trade Policy	Professional Investor
Exchange Rates	Geopolitical Conflict	Forecasts
Foreign Trade		

Economic Drivers   Economic drivers are anything related to the macroeconomic environment. This could include monetary policy, interest rates, lending activity, yield curve analysis, relative GDP growth analysis, and myriad others. What economic forces are likely to drive GDP growth throughout countries in the world? What is the outlook for interest rates, and how would that impact sectors? What is the outlook for Telecom and infrastructure spending among countries?

Economic drivers pertain not only to the fundamental outlook of the economy (GDP growth, interest rates, inflation), but also to the stock market (valuations, M&A activity, share buybacks). As an investor, it's your job to identify these drivers and determine how they'll impact your overall portfolio and each of its segments.

Following is a list of sample economic drivers that could impact portfolio performance:

- US economic growth will be higher than consensus expectations.
- European Union interest rates will remain benign.
- Mergers, acquisitions, and share buybacks will be strong.
- Emerging markets growth will drive commodity demand.

Political Drivers   Political drivers can be country-specific, pertain to regions (European Union, Organisation for Economic Co-operation and Development [OECD]), or affect interaction between countries or regions (such as trade policies). These drivers are more concerned with categories such as taxation, government stability, fiscal policy, and political turnover. Which countries are experiencing a change in government that could have a meaningful impact on their economies? Which sectors could be at risk from new taxation or legislation? Which countries are undergoing pro-growth reforms?

Political drivers will help determine the relative attractiveness of market segments and countries based on the outlook for the political environment. Be warned, however: Most investors suffer from "home country bias," ascribing too much importance to the politics of their own country. Always keep in mind it's a big, interconnected world out there, and geopolitical developments everywhere can have implications.

What are possible political drivers you can find? The following is a list of examples that can drive stocks up or down.

- Political party change in Japan driving pro-growth reforms.
- New tax policies in Germany stalling economic growth.
- Protests, government coups, and conflict driving political instability in Thailand.

Sentiment Drivers   Sentiment drivers attempt to measure consensus thinking about investment categories. Ideally, drivers identify market opportunities where sentiment is different from reality. For example, let's say you observe current broad market sentiment that expects a US recession in the next year. But you disagree and believe GDP growth will be strong. This presents an excellent opportunity for excess returns. You can load up on stocks that will benefit from an economic boom and watch the prices rise as the rest of the market realizes it much later.

Because the market is a discounter of all known information, it's important to try to identify what the market is pricing in. The interpretation of such investor drivers is typically counterintuitive (avoid what is overly popular and seek what is largely unpopular). Looking forward, which sectors are investors most bullish about and why? What countries or sectors are widely discussed in the media? What market segments have been bid up recently based on something other than fundamentals? If the market's perception is different from fundamentals in the short term, stocks will eventually correct themselves to reflect reality in the long term.

A note of caution: Gauging market sentiment does not mean being a contrarian. Contrarians are investors who simply do the opposite of what most believe will happen. Instead, find places where sentiment (people's beliefs) doesn't match what you believe is reality, and overweight- or underweight portions of your portfolio relative to your benchmark accordingly. Examples of sentiment drivers include:

- Investors remain pessimistic about Telecom despite improving fundamentals.
- Sentiment for the Chinese stock market approaches euphoria, stretching valuations.
- Professional investors universally forecast US small cap stocks to outperform.

How to Create Your Own Investment Drivers

The first step in determining your own investment drivers is accessing a wide array of data from multiple sources. For country drivers, this could range from globally focused publications like *The Wall Street Journal* or *Financial Times* to regional newspapers or government data. For sector drivers, this could include reading trade publications or following major company announcements.

Remember, however, that markets are efficient—they reflect all widely known information. Most pertinent information about public companies is, well, public. Which means the market already knows. News travels fast, and knowledge and expectations are absorbed by markets quickly. Those seeking to profit on a bit of news, rumor, or speculation must acknowledge the market will probably move faster than they can. Therefore, in order to consistently generate excess returns, you must either know something others don't or interpret widely known information differently and correctly from the crowd. (For a detailed discussion on these factors and more, read *The Only Three Questions That Count*, by Ken Fisher.)

Step 2: Quantitative Factor Screening

Step two in the top-down method is screening for quantitative factors. This allows you to narrow the potential list of stocks once your portfolio drivers are in place.

There are thousands and thousands of stocks out there, so it's vital to use a series of factors like market capitalization and valuations to narrow the field a bit. Securities passing this screen are then subjected to further quantitative analysis that eliminates companies with extreme risk profiles relative to their peer group, such as companies with excessive leverage or balance sheet risk and securities lacking sufficient liquidity for investment.

The rigidity of the quantitative screens is entirely up to you and will determine the number of companies on your prospect list. The more rigid the criteria, the fewer the companies that make the list. Broader criteria will increase the number of companies.

Examples   How can you perform such a screen? Here are two examples of quantitative factor screenings to show how broad or specific you can be. You might want to apply strict criteria, or you may prefer to be broader.

Strict Criteria

- First, you decide you want to search for only Telecommunications firms. By definition, that excludes all companies from the other nine sectors. Already, you've narrowed the field a lot!
- Now, let's say that based on your high-level drivers, you only want European Telecommunications stocks. By excluding all other regions besides Europe, you've narrowed the field even more.
- Next, let's decide to search only for Integrated firms in the Telecommunications sector.
- Perhaps you don't believe small stocks are preferable, so you limit market capitalization to $3 billion and above.

- Last, let's set some parameters for valuation:
  - P/E (price-to-earnings) less than 14x
  - P/B (price-to-book) less than 2x
  - P/CF (price-to-cash-flow) less than 10x
  - P/S (price-to-sales) less than 3x

This rigorous process of selecting parameters will yield a small number of stocks to research, all based on your higher-level themes. But maybe you have reason to be less specific and want to do a broader screen because you think Telecommunications in general is a good place to be. A broad screen might have only the following criteria:

- Telecommunications sector
- Global (no country or region restrictions)
- Market caps above $1 billion

This selection process is much broader and obviously gives you a much longer list of stocks to choose from. Neither a strict nor a broad screen is inherently better. It just depends on how well-formed and specific your higher-level themes are. Obviously, a stricter screen means less work for you in step three—actual stock selection.

Step 3: Stock Selection

After narrowing the prospect list, your final step is identifying individual securities possessing strategic attributes consistent with higher-level portfolio themes. (We'll cover the stock selection process specifically in more detail in Chapter 8.) Your stock selection process should attempt to accomplish two goals:

1. Seek firms possessing strategic attributes consistent with higher-level portfolio themes derived from the drivers that give those firms a competitive advantage over their peers. For example, if you believe owning firms with dominant market shares in consolidating industries is a favorable characteristic, you would search for firms with that profile.

2. Seek to maximize the likelihood of beating the category of stocks you are analyzing. For example, if you want a certain portfolio weight of Wireless companies and need 4 stocks out of 12 meeting the quantitative criteria, you then pick the 4 that, as a group, maximize the likelihood of beating all 12 as a whole. This is different from trying to pick "the best four." By avoiding stocks likely to be extreme or "weird" outliers versus the group, you can reduce portfolio risk while adding value at the security selection level.

In lieu of picking individual securities, you can use other ways to exploit high-level themes in the top-down process. For instance, if you feel strongly about a particular sub-industry but don't think you can add value through individual security analysis, it may be more prudent to buy a group of companies in the sub-industry or a category product like an exchange-traded fund (ETF). A growing variety of ETFs track the domestic and global Telecommunications sector, industries, and even specific commodity prices. This way, you can be sure to gain broad Telecommunications exposure without much stock-specific risk. (For more information on ETFs, visit www.ishares .com, www.sectorspdr.com, or www.masterdata.com.)

MANAGING AGAINST A TELECOMMUNICATIONS BENCHMARK

Now we can practice translating this specifically to your Telecommunications allocation. Just as you analyze the components of your benchmark to determine country and sector components in a top-down strategy, you must analyze each sector's components, as we did in Chapter 3. To demonstrate how, we'll use the MSCI World Telecommunications Sector Index as the benchmark. Table 7.5 shows the MSCI World Telecommunications sub-industry weights as of December 31, 2009. We don't know what the sample portfolio weights should be, but we know it should add up to 100 percent. Of course, if managing against a broader benchmark, your

Table 7.5   MSCI World Telecommunications Sub-Industry Weights Versus Sample Portfolio

Industry	MSCI World (%)	Sample Portfolio
Integrated Services	69%	?
Alternative Carriers	1%	?
Wireless Services	30%	?
Total	**100%**	**100%**

Source: Thomson Reuters; MSCI, Inc.,[7] MSCI World Index as of 12/31/08.

Telecommunications sector weight may add up to more or less than the Telecommunications weight in the benchmark, depending on over- or underweight decisions.

Keeping the sub-industry weights in mind will help mitigate benchmark risk. If you have a portfolio of stocks with the same sub-industry weights as the MSCI World Telecommunications Index, you're neutral—taking no benchmark risk. However, if you feel strongly about a sub-industry, like Alternative Carriers and decide to purchase only those firms (one of the smallest weights in the sector), you're taking a huge benchmark risk. The same is true if you significantly underweight a sub-industry. All the same rules apply as when you do this from a broader portfolio perspective, as we did earlier in this chapter.

The benchmark's sub-industry weights provide a jumping-off point in making further portfolio decisions. After you make higher-level decisions on the sub-industries, you can make choices versus the benchmark by overweighting the sub-industries you feel are likeliest to perform best and underweighting those likeliest to perform worst. Table 7.6 shows how you can make different portfolio bets against the benchmark by over- and underweighting sub-industries. *Note: Portfolio A might be a portfolio of all Telecommunications stocks, or it can simply represent a neutral Telecommunications sector allocation in a larger portfolio.)*

The "difference" column shows the relative difference between the benchmark and Portfolio A. In this example, Portfolio A is most overweight to Wireless Services and most underweight to Integrated Services.

Table 7.6   Portfolio A

Industry	MSCI World (%)	Sample Portfolio	Difference
Integrated Services	69%	64%	−5%
Alternative Carriers	1%	3%	2%
Wireless Services	30%	33%	3%
Total	**100%**	**100%**	**0%**

Source: Thomson Reuters; MSCI, Inc.,[8] MSCI World Index as of 12/31/08.

In other words, for this hypothetical example, Portfolio A's owner expects Wireless and Alternative Carriers to outperform the sector and Integrated Services to underperform the sector. But in terms of benchmark risk, Portfolio A remains fairly close to the benchmark weights, so its relative risk is quite modest. This is extremely important: By managing against a benchmark, you can make strategic choices to beat the index and be well-diversified within the sector without concentrating too heavily in a specific area.

Table 7.7 is another example of relative portfolio weighting versus the benchmark. Portfolio B is significantly underweight to Wireless Services with exposure concentrated in Integrated Services. Because the sub-industry weights are so different from the benchmark, Portfolio B takes on substantially more relative risk than Portfolio A.

Regardless of how your portfolio is positioned relative to the benchmark, it's important to use benchmarks to identify where your relative risks are before investing. Knowing the benchmark weights

Table 7.7   Portfolio B

Industry	MSCI World (%)	Sample Portfolio	Difference
Integrated Services	69%	91%	22%
Alternative Carriers	1%	2%	1%
Wireless Services	30%	7%	−23%
Total	**100%**	**100%**	**0%**

Source: Thomson Reuters; MSCI, Inc.,[9] MSCI World Index as of 12/31/08.

and having opinions on the future performance of each sub-industry are crucial steps in building a portfolio designed to beat the benchmark. Should you make the correct overweight and underweight decisions, you're likelier to beat the benchmark regardless of the individual securities held within. But even if you're wrong, you'll have diversified enough not to lose your shirt.

Chapter Recap

An effective approach to sector analysis is "top-down." A top-down investment methodology analyzes big picture factors such as economics, politics, and sentiment to forecast which investment categories are likely to outperform the market. A key part of the process is the use of benchmarks (such as the MSCI World Telecommunications or S&P 500 Telecommunications indexes) as guidelines for building portfolios, monitoring performance, and managing risk. By analyzing portfolio drivers, we can identify which Telecommunications industries and sub-industries are most attractive and unattractive, ultimately filtering down to stock selection.

- The top-down investment methodology first identifies and analyzes high-level portfolio drivers affecting broad categories of stocks. These drivers help determine portfolio country, sector, and style weights. The same methodology can be applied to a specific sector to determine industry and sub-industry weights.

- Quantitative factor screening helps narrow the list of potential portfolio holdings based on characteristics such as valuations, liquidity, and solvency.

- Stock selection is the final step in the top-down process. Stock selection attempts to find companies possessing strategic attributes consistent with higher-level portfolio drivers.

- Stock selection also attempts to find companies with the greatest probability of outperforming their peers.

- It's helpful to use a Telecommunications benchmark as a guide when constructing a portfolio to determine your sub-industry overweights and underweights.

8

SECURITY ANALYSIS

Now that we've covered the top-down method, let's pick some stocks. This chapter walks you through analyzing individual Telecommunications firms using the top-down method presented in Chapter 7. Specifically, we demonstrate a five-step process for analyzing firms relative to peers.

Every firm and every stock is different, and viewing them through the right lens is vital. Investors need a functional, consistent, and reusable framework for analyzing securities across the sector. Though by no means comprehensive, the framework provided and the questions at this chapter's end should serve as good starting points to help identify strategic attributes and company-specific risks.

Volumes have been written about individual security analysis, but a top-down investment approach de-emphasizes the importance of stock selection in a portfolio. As such, we talk about the basics of stock analysis for the beginner-to-intermediate investor. For a more thorough understanding of financial statement analysis, valuations, modeling, and other tools of security analysis, additional reading is suggested.

Top-Down Recap

As covered in Chapter 7, you can use the top-down method to make your biggest, most important portfolio decisions first. However, the same process applies when picking stocks, and those high-level portfolio decisions ultimately filter down to individual securities.

Step one is analyzing the broader global economy and identifying various macro "drivers" affecting entire sectors or industries. Using the drivers, you can make general allocation decisions for countries, sectors, industries, and sub-industries versus the given benchmark. Step two is applying quantitative screening criteria to narrow the choice set of stocks. It's not until all those decisions are made that we get to analyze individual stocks. Security analysis is the third and final step.

For the rest of the chapter, we assume you have already established a benchmark, solidified portfolio themes, made sub-industry overweight and underweight decisions, and are ready to analyze firms within a peer group. (A peer group is a group of stocks you'd generally expect to perform similarly because they operate in the same industry, possibly share the same geography, and have similar quantitative attributes.)

MAKE YOUR SELECTION

Security analysis is nowhere near as complicated as it may seem—but that doesn't mean it's easy. As with your goal in choosing industry and sector weights, you've got one basic task: spot opportunities not currently discounted into prices. Or, put differently, know something others don't. Investors should analyze firms by taking consensus expectations for a company's estimated financial results and then assessing whether it will perform below, in line with, or above those baseline expectations. Profit opportunities arise when your expectations are different and more accurate than consensus expectations. Trading on widely known information or consensus expectations adds no value to the stock selection process. Doing so is really no different from trading on a coin flip.

The top-down method offers two ways to spot such opportunities. First, accurately predict high-level, macro themes affecting an industry or group of companies—these are your portfolio drivers. Second, find firms that will benefit most if those high-level themes and drivers play out. This is done by finding firms with competitive advantages (we'll explain this concept more in a bit).

Because the majority of excess return is added in higher-level decisions in the top-down process, it's not vital to pick the "best" stocks in the universe. Rather, you want to pick stocks with a good probability of outperforming their peers. Doing so can enhance returns without jeopardizing good top-down decisions by picking risky, go-big-or-go-home stocks. Being right more often than not should create outperformance relative to the benchmark over time.

A FIVE-STEP PROCESS

Analyzing a stock against its peer group can be summarized as a five-step process:

1. Understand business and earnings drivers.
2. Identify strategic attributes.
3. Analyze fundamental and stock price performance.
4. Identify risks.
5. Analyze valuations and consensus expectations.

These five steps provide a consistent framework for analyzing firms in their peer groups. While these steps are far from a full stock analysis, they provide the basics necessary to begin making better stock selections.

Step 1: Understand Business and Earnings Drivers

The first step is to understand what the business does, how it generates its earnings, and what drives those earnings. Here are a few tips to help in the process.

- **Industry overview.** Begin any analysis with a basic understanding of the firm's industry, including its drivers and risks. You should be familiar with how current economic trends affect the industry.

- **Company description.** Obtain a business description of the company, including an understanding of the products and services within each business segment. It's always best to go directly to a company's financial statements for this. (Almost every public firm makes their financial statements readily accessible online these days.) Browse the firm's website and financial reports to gain an overview of the company and how it presents itself.

- **Corporate history.** Read the firm's history since its inception and over the last several years. An understanding of firm history may reveal its growth strategy or consistency with success and failure. It also will provide clues on what its true core competencies are. Ask questions like: Has it been an industry leader for decades, or is it a relative newcomer? Has it switched strategies or businesses often in the past?

- **Business segments.** Break down company revenues and earnings by business segment and geography to determine how and where it makes its money. Find out what drives results in each business and geographic segment. Begin thinking about how each of these business segments fits into your high-level themes.

- **Recent news and press releases.** Read all recently released news about the stock, including press releases. Do a Google search and see what comes up. Look for any significant announcements regarding company operations. What's the media's opinion of the firm? Is it a bellwether to the industry or a minor player?

- **Markets and customers.** Identify main customers and the markets it operates in. Determine whether the firm has any particularly large single customer or a concentrated customer base.

- **Competition.** Find the main competitors and how market share compares with other industry players. Is the industry highly segmented? Assess the industry's competitive landscape. Keep in mind the biggest competitors can sometimes lurk in different industries—sometimes even in different sectors! Get a feel for how the firm stacks up—is it an industry leader or a minor player? Does market share matter in that industry?

Step 2: Identify Strategic Attributes

After gaining a firm grasp of firm operations, the next step is identifying strategic attributes consistent with higher-level portfolio themes. Also known as competitive or comparative advantages, strategic attributes are unique features allowing firms to outperform their industry or sector. Because industry peers are generally affected by the same high-level drivers, strong strategic attributes are the edge in creating superior performance. Examples of strategic attributes include:

- Favorable regulatory regime
- High relative market share
- Low-cost production
- Superior sales relationships/distribution
- Economic sensitivity
- Vertical integration
- Strong management/business strategy
- Geographic diversity or advantage
- Consolidator
- Strong balance sheet
- Niche market exposure

Strategic Attributes: Making Lemonade

How do strategic attributes help you analyze individual stocks? Consider a simple example: There are five lemonade stands of similar size, product, and quality within a city block. A scorching heat wave envelops the city, sending a rush of customers in search of lemonade. Which stand benefits most from the industry-wide surge in business? This likely depends on each stand's strategic attributes. Maybe one is a cost leader and has cheapest access to homegrown lemons. Maybe one has a geographic advantage and is located next to a basketball court full of thirsty players. Or maybe one has a superior business strategy with a "buy two, get one free" initiative that drives higher sales volume and a bigger customer base. Any of these are core strategic advantages.

- Pure play
- Potential takeover target
- Proprietary technologies
- Strong brand name
- First mover advantage

Portfolio drivers help determine which strategic attributes are likely to face head- or tailwinds. After all, not all strategic attributes will benefit a firm in all environments. For example, while higher operating leverage might help a firm boost earnings in the booming part of an industry, it would have the opposite effect in a down cycle.

A pertinent example in the Telecom sector is a diversified service provider. During periods of high user additions, the company's low variable costs allow it to earn wide margins. However, when competition is fierce and customer churn is high, the service provider's high fixed costs may be a headwind. Thus, it's essential to pick strategic attributes consistent with higher-level portfolio themes and analyze the ones that may be more important in the current environment.

A strategic attribute is also only effective to the extent management recognizes and takes advantage of it. Execution is key. For example, a telco may be strategically positioned in a geographic region with demand growth, but it can only capitalize on this advantage if it has access to the capital to make the investments necessary to meet this demand.

Identifying strategic attributes may require thorough research of a firm's financial statements, website, news stories, history, and discussions with customers, suppliers, competitors, or management. Don't skimp on this step—be diligent and thorough in finding strategic attributes. It may feel an arduous task at times, but it's also among the most important in security selection.

Step 3: Analyze Fundamental and Stock Price Performance

After you've gained a thorough understanding of the business, earnings drivers, and strategic attributes, the next step is analyzing firm performance both fundamentally and in the stock market. Using the latest earnings releases, annual reports, and the company's conference calls with financial analysts, first analyze the company's recent financial performance. Ask the following questions:

- What are recent trends for revenues, margins, and earnings? What business activities are driving results, and how?
- Have earnings tended to be above or below company guidance? How did earnings compare to consensus estimates?
- Are earnings growing because of higher volumes, higher prices, or lower costs?
- Are headline earnings affected by one-off accounting items?
- Were there any major regulatory events? How might they impact future financial performance?
- Is the company growing organically, because of acquisitions, or for some other reason?
- Is the company generating sufficient operating cash flow to fund its capital investments? If not, how is it financing the difference? Can the company obtain capital at attractive rates?
- What is management's strategy for the future? Will management invest in growth or return excess capital to shareholders?
- How sustainable is the strategy? Is it predicated on realistic macroeconomic assumptions?
- What is the financial health of the company? Does it have sufficient liquidity to meet its financial obligations?

After familiarizing yourself with the company, evaluate some of its peers. You'll begin to notice similar trends and events affecting the broader industry. Take note of these so you can distinguish between issues that are company-specific and those that are industry-wide.

Once you've got a sense of the company's fundamental financial performance, check the company's stock chart for the last few years. In light of the financial statements you've reviewed, does the stock chart look like what you would expect?

Explain any big up or down moves in the company's share price, and identify any significant news events. If the stock price has trended steadily downward despite ostensibly strong financial performance, the market may be discounting an expected future event—perhaps the market is expecting a negative outcome in future regulation changes.

Or if the company's share price has soared despite weak financial performance, there may be some unseen force driving shares higher, such as speculation the company may be a takeover target. Sometimes, stock-specific financial performance may be overshadowed by broad industry trends, such as rising interest rates or changes in regulation. Or stocks can simply move in sympathy with the broader market. Whatever it is, make sure you know.

Step 4: Identify Risks

There are two main types of risks in security analysis: stock-specific risk and systematic risk (also known as non-stock specific risk). Both can be equally important to performance.

Stock-specific risks, as the name suggests, are issues affecting the company in isolation. These are mainly risks affecting a firm's business operations or future operations. Some company-specific risks are discussed in detail in the 10-K for US firms and the 20-F for foreign filers (found at www.sec.gov). But one can't rely solely on firms self-identifying risk factors. You must see what analysts are saying about them and identify all risks for yourself. Some examples include:

- Regulatory proceedings
- High earnings sensitivity to commodity prices
- Customer concentration
- Supply chain risks
- Excessive leverage or lack of access to financing
- Poor operational track record
- High cost relative to competitors
- Late SEC filings
- Qualified audit opinions
- Hedging or trading activities
- Pension or benefit underfunding risk

- Outstanding litigation
- Pending corporate actions
- Executive departures
- Stock ownership concentration (insider or institutional)

Systematic risks include macroeconomic or geopolitical events out of a company's control. While the risks may affect a broad set of firms, they will have varying effects on each. Some examples include:

- Economic activity
- Commodity prices
- Interest rates
- Industry cost inflation
- Supply chain disruptions
- Legislative risk
- Geopolitical risks
- Weather

Identifying stock-specific risks helps an investor evaluate the relative risk and reward potential of firms within a peer group. Identifying systematic risks helps you make informed decisions about which sub-industries and countries to overweight or underweight.

If you don't feel strongly about any company in a peer group within a sub-industry you wish to overweight, you could pick the company with the least stock-specific risk. This would help to achieve the goal of picking firms with the greatest probability of outperforming their peer group but still performing in line with your higher-level themes and drivers.

Step 5: Analyze Valuations and Consensus Expectations

Valuations can be tricky things. They are tools used to evaluate market sentiment and expectations for firms. They are not a foolproof way to see if a stock is "cheap" or "expensive." For example, most Telecom firms have lower price to earnings than most Information Technology (IT) companies, but that doesn't necessarily make the sector a better value—IT companies earn their premium valuation by providing higher returns on capital and growth rates.

Investors are usually best served by comparing a firm's valuation to that of its peer group or relative to its own historical average. Investors use many different valuation metrics in security analysis. Most look at companies' current share prices relative to some financial metric—either based on historical performance or future expectations. Some of the most popular include:

- P/E—price to earnings
- P/B—price to book
- P/S—price to sales
- P/CF—price to cash flow
- DY—dividend yield
- EV/EBITDA—enterprise value to earnings before interest, taxes, depreciation, and amortization

Even within a peer group, relative valuations in and of themselves do not provide insight into future stock performance. Just because one company's P/E is 20 while another's is 10 doesn't mean you should necessarily buy the one at 10 because it's "cheaper." When valuations are different, there's usually a reason, such as different strategic attributes, growth and profitability expectations, or stock-specific risks. The main question for investors is thus, "Are valuations justified by fundamentals?" To answer this question, compile the valuations for a peer group and try to estimate why there are relative differences in valuation. Often, there's a strong relationship between valuations and financial performance.

However, valuations are not determined solely by a single financial metric. There are other, more qualitative factors which may provide a company with a higher—or lower—valuation than its financial performance might imply. For example, if a telco is in the midst of a contentious proceeding with its regulator, investors may assign a valuation multiple which is lower than its financial performance might otherwise imply. Or perhaps investors speculate the telco is a viable takeover target and provide a higher premium.

Once you understand the reasons for a telco's relative valuation, you can then attempt to determine whether it's justified. For example, perhaps you find a company which has a low valuation because of an expected dividend cut. If your analysis leads you to believe analyst earnings expectations are too conservative, you might conclude the company's dividend will be higher than expected, and thus the company's valuation multiple will expand.

Ultimately, valuations tell you what other investors think about a company's current and future prospects. Because stocks trade on the unexpected, understanding what investors expect is critical since it allows you to determine whether you believe reality will turn out to be better or worse than expected.

TELECOM ANALYSIS

This chapter's framework can be used to analyze any firm, but there are additional factors specific to the Telecom sector that must be considered. The following section provides some of the most important factors and questions to think about when researching firms in the sector. Answers to these questions should help distinguish between firms within a peer group and help identify strategic attributes and stock-specific risks. And while there are countless other questions and factors that could and should be asked when researching Telecom firms, these should serve as a good starting point.

> **Product mix.** It is important to know if a company is levered to products in a growing or shrinking category. How many fixed lines does the company have in service? Are they residential or business lines? What's the mix of wireline to wireless revenue? What's the mix of prepaid and postpaid mobile subscribers? Does the company have an advantage in its handset offerings? How many broadband subscribers are there?
>
> **Subscription trends.** Wireline and wireless subscriber trends can often tell you how well a company is doing in the end markets it serves. What were the subscriber retention and churn rates?

What were the gross and net additions? What was the gross cost per addition? How do these metrics compare to peers?

Average revenue per user (ARPU). Ideally, you want to invest in a company in which ARPU is rising. If ARPU isn't rising, why isn't it? Is it because of usage, pricing, or both? Was an increase or decrease in ARPU driven by data or voice services?

Sales growth. Net sales growth is a positive sign for a business, but as a stock analyst you must determine how top-line sales growth is derived if you are to determine the quality of the sales growth. Was the top line influenced primarily by acquisitions or divestitures, or was it organic growth from ongoing operations? You can extrapolate organic growth into the future with more confidence than you can acquisition-based growth, so it is generally considered a more relevant analytic.

Geographic diversity. How wide is the firm's geographic reach? Does the firm have meaningful exposure to high-growth international markets? Is the firm concentrated in a slow-growth, mature market? Geographic diversification can help smooth earnings trends, as growth in one market can offset weakness in other markets. If a company is expanding internationally, what are the region's penetration rates, and what do margins look like in those markets? For internationally diversified firms, keep in mind fluctuations in foreign currency values influence the way sales and earnings are reported in US dollars.

Competition and barriers to entry. What does the competitive landscape look like? Are there firmly entrenched market share leaders who are insulated from smaller competitors via high barriers to entry? Are there substitutes for the company's products or services?

Margins. Are margins growing or shrinking? And what is driving this movement? Has the company historically offset higher costs with higher prices? How do its margins compare to those of peers?

Business strategy. Has the company recently been acquiring or divesting businesses? If so, what are the drivers behind such activity? If the company is a consolidator, does it have a successful track record of creating positive synergies like increased operating leverage, capacity utilization, and distribution network efficiencies? If a firm is in divestment mode, what were the catalysts, and what is the strategy looking forward? Is it moving into higher growth categories?

Management. What is management's reputation? Is a seasoned team in place with a strong track record of building the business and adding shareholder value? Have they executed on stated goals and met their guidance to Wall Street? Has there been management turnover?

Brand equity. Is the brand highly recognizable and respected? What are the firm's strategies in promoting the brand? A well-respected brand gives a firm the ability to price its product above the competition and to more easily expand into new geographic regions.

Political risk. Telecommunications and politics are closely tied together, and legislative changes can occur on a relatively frequent basis. Does the firm currently operate in a favorable regulatory environment? How does it compare to other geographic regions? How might regulation change?

Financial strength. Does the company have enough cash and cash flows to operate well into the future? Compare the firm's interest costs with the amount of operating income the business generates (interest coverage ratio). Will the firm require additional funds in the future to expand its operation? If so, is there capacity to take on more debt, or would the firm have to engage in an equity offering that may dilute existing shareholders? You can investigate financial health by comparing balance sheet financial ratios to peers. Ratios such as long-term debt to capital and the current ratio can be used to assess a firm's capitalization structure and level of liquidity. Comparing credit ratings to peers is another tool at your disposal. The primary ratings agencies include Standard & Poor's, Moody's, and Fitch.

Recall debt isn't necessarily a bad thing when defining financial strength—many firms generate an excellent return on borrowed funds. Understanding the capital structure of a firm and its history of generating returns on capital will help you appraise the optimal level of debt.

Dividend yield. Confidence in the sustainability of a company's cash flow and dividends is crucial. How stable do they appear? What's the company's payout ratio (dividend/net income)? Although there's no rule, if it's less than 0.7, it's probably less likely to be cut than a peer with a higher ratio.

Reinvestments. If a company's payout ratio is low, it may mean the company is investing a higher percentage of profits in future growth. Often, earnings growth is fueled by capital expenditures (capex) to increase coverage and capacity. How much of sales are capex? How efficient does the company's spending appear to be? What's the capex efficiency ratio (EBITDA/capex)? How do these ratios compare to peers'?

Create Your Own Metric

We have covered common industry factors, but with a little creativity, you can come up with your own. For example, if you're interested in finding stocks that aren't too volatile and have a high dividend yield, create a yield/beta ratio. The company with the greatest yield per unit of beta may be an easy way to compare companies and identify a superior investment.

Chapter Recap

Security analysis is not nearly as complicated as it seems. In the top-down investment process, stocks are essentially tools we use to take advantage of opportunities we identify in higher-level themes. After identifying an attractive segment of the market, we attempt to determine the firms most likely to outperform their peers by finding firms with strategic attributes. While the five-step security selection process is just one of many ways to research firms, it is an effective framework for selecting securities within the top-down process.

When researching Telecom firms, do not limit yourself to the questions posed in this chapter; they are just some tools that can help you distinguish between firms. The more questions you ask, the better your analysis will be.

- Stock selection, the third and final step in the top-down investment process, attempts to identify securities that will benefit from our high-level portfolio themes.

- Ultimately, stock selection attempts to spot opportunities not currently discounted into prices.

- To identify firms most likely to outperform their peer group, we must find firms that possess competitive advantages (aka strategic attributes).

- A five-step security selection process can be used as a framework to research firms.

- Firms within each industry have specific characteristics and strategies separating potential winners from losers. Asking the right questions can help identify those features.

9

TELECOM
INVESTING STRATEGIES

This chapter covers various investing strategies specifically for a Telecom allocation, building on the knowledge presented in this book. The strategies include:

- Adding value at the sector level
- Adding value at the country or industry level
- Adding value at the security level

Although the strategies presented here are by no means comprehensive, they provide a good starting point to construct a portfolio that can increase your likelihood of outperforming a benchmark. They should also help spur some investment strategy ideas of your own. After all, using this framework to discover information few others have discovered yet is what investing is all about.

Also, these strategies may focus solely on Telecom, but they are meant to be used as part of an overarching strategy for a portfolio managed against a broader benchmark. Some investors may choose to manage a portfolio of only Telecom stocks (or any other single sector). But in our view, for individual investors, managing against a broader benchmark increases both risk management and outperformance opportunities.

STRATEGY 1: ADDING VALUE AT THE SECTOR LEVEL

Consistent with the top-down method, investors must first determine when it is appropriate to overweight or underweight the Telecom sector relative to a broader portfolio benchmark. Some major factors contributing to this decision, covered in depth in Chapter 4, are shown in Table 9.1. Each driver should be considered not on its own, but in combination with other relevant drivers and also larger macroeconomic conditions. Also, don't take this table to mean overweight decisions can be driven by the mere number of positive drivers (and the same is true in reverse with underweight decisions). At any one time, there can be many more meaningful drivers than we have space to list here. And some drivers are more important than others. The most important macroeconomic drivers can swamp sector, industry, and sub-industry drivers.

Implementing Sector Overweights and Underweights

After the decision is made to overweight or underweight the sector, it's time to implement it. The first step is determining the sector weight

Table 9.1   When to Overweight and Underweight the Telecom Sector

Driver/Factor	Bullish	Bearish
Economic Growth	Slowing	Accelerating
Interest Rates	Falling	Rising
Regulatory Environment	Certain	Uncertain
Risk Aversion	High	Low
Style Leadership	Value	Growth
Size Leadership	Large	Small

relative to your benchmark. The relative bet size should be proportional to your conviction. Mild conviction should translate to a more modest bet against the benchmark. The stronger your conviction, the bigger your bet can be—within reason. A vital rule is to never make a bet so large that if you're wrong, you inflict irreparable damage on your portfolio's return versus the benchmark.

Next comes determining the actual investments. One method is completely mimicking the sector by buying all the sector's stocks in direct proportion to your under- or overweight. Obviously, this can be time consuming and costly—particularly for individual investors working with relatively smaller pools of money—depending on the number of stocks. An easier and likely cheaper method of mimicking the sector composition is buying exchange traded funds (ETFs) or mutual funds. The following are some larger Telecom ETFs and their stock tickers (again, this list is by no means exhaustive):

- Dow Jones US Telecommunications Sector Index Fund (IYZ)
- S&P Global Telecommunications Sector Index Fund (IXP)
- Merrill Lynch Telecom HOLDRs (TTH)
- Merrill Lynch Wireless HOLDRs (WMH)
- Vanguard Telecommunication Services ETF (VOX)
- PowerShares Dynamic Telecommunications & Wireless Portfolio (PTE)
- SPDR S&P International Telecommunications Sector (IST)

STRATEGY 2: ADDING VALUE AT THE COUNTRY OR INDUSTRY LEVEL

A more advanced strategy is making country- and industry-level bets based on your top-down analysis. Each Telecom industry and region falls in and out of favor periodically—no one area outperforms consistently over the long term. Your job is to determine how pronounced the degree of leading or lagging will be, when it's likeliest to happen, and whether it's likely to be profitable enough to make a bet.

Chapters 5 and 6 should provide a structure for asking relevant questions to assist such decisions. For example, Chapter 5 outlines key variables for identifying trends in wireline and wireless firms, such as:

- What countries, regions, and industries have the best prospects based on penetration rates and disposable income?
- What will drive wireline and wireless performance? Voice, data, or both?
- What are the most popular services driving demand for wireline and wireless data consumption? Are they likely to continue?

After such questions are answered, they should be scrutinized by examining appropriate challenges and opportunities as exemplified in Chapter 6. Ultimately, your decision to overweight or underweight an industry relative to the benchmark should jibe with your high-level portfolio drivers. Note: *Always remember past performance is no guarantee of future performance.* No set of rules works for all time, and you should always analyze the entire situation before investing. The past is about understanding context and precedent for investing—it's not a roadmap for the future.

STRATEGY 3: ADDING VALUE AT THE SECURITY LEVEL

A still more advanced strategy entails investing directly in individual firms. This strategy should be based on your sector, country, and industry opinions—and was covered in more depth in Chapter 8. Never forget, individual stock selection should be driven by higher level, top-down portfolio themes. For example, if you have a strong conviction the developed world is entering a period of robust overall growth, you know that is typically a period when Telecom stocks tend to underperform (though not always). And if Telecom overall underperforms, even the best stock picking in the world means your Telecom selections are likely to lag better-performing sector stocks on an *absolute* basis.

Table 9.2   Examples of Top-Down Security Selection

Hypothesis	Area of Focus	Possible Candidates
US interest rates will continue to fall	US telcos with stable and high dividend yields	AT&T, Verizon
Increasing wealth in the EMs should fuel consumer spending and wireless telecom growth	Regions like China and India with relatively strong economic growth and low wireless penetration rates	China Mobile, Bharti Airtel
Smartphone adoption will continue at a brisk pace	Wireless companies in developed markets with 3G or 4G networks	Vodafone, NTT DoCoMo

However, in a period when Telecom underperforms, if you pick stocks well, your overall sector allocation may perform as well or better than your sector benchmark—which can help your overall *relative* performance. And during periods when Telecom does perform better than the overall market, if you can add value at the security level, you can improve your portfolio performance both on an absolute and a relative basis.

In Table 9.2, we provide examples of strategies for top-down security selection—though there are countless others. Further, the stocks named are just a few of those that, as of this writing, are emblematic of the higher-level themes we're trying to capture based on the hypothesis. As you become more familiar with specific Telecom firms and their industries, you can eventually develop your own strategies. Always be vigilant for firm-specific issues that could cause a stock to act differently from what you would expect in the context of your broader strategy.

Chapter Recap

We couldn't possibly list every investment strategy out there for the Telecom sector. Different strategies will work best at different times. Some will become obsolete. New ones will be discovered. Whatever

(Continued)

strategies you choose, always know you could be wrong! Decisions to significantly overweight or underweight an industry relative to the benchmark should be based on a multitude of factors, including an assessment of risk. The point of benchmarking is to properly diversify, so make sure you always have counterstrategies built into your portfolio.

- There are numerous ways to invest in the Telecom sector. These include investing in ETFs, index or mutual funds, or buying the stocks themselves.

- Investors can enhance returns by overweighting and underweighting industries or countries based on a variety of high-level drivers.

- An advanced strategy involves making bets on individual stocks based on specific themes.

Appendix
Additional Resources

This appendix provides additional sources of data and information that may be useful in crafting a forward-looking assessment of the Telecom sector. Although most major Telecom developments are covered in mainstream business newspapers like *The Wall Street Journal*, the sites listed in this appendix provide opportunities to obtain more detailed information. This list is by no means exhaustive but includes some of the more common sites you are likely to use.

Industry Associations

CDMA Development Group (CDG)

www.cdg.org

CDG is an international consortium of companies that jointly define the technical requirements for the evolution of CDMA2000 and complementary 4G systems, as well as interoperability with other emerging wireless technologies.

COMPTEL

www.comptel.org

COMPTEL represents communications service providers and their supplier partners. COMPTEL advances its members' interests through trade shows, networking, education, and policy advocacy before Congress, the Federal Communications Commission, and the courts.

CTIA—The Wireless Association

www.ctia.org

CTIA is an international nonprofit membership organization that represents the wireless communications industry. It advocates on behalf of its members at all levels of government.

GSM Association

www.gsmworld.com

GSMA is an association of mobile operators and related companies devoted to supporting the standardization, deployment, and promotion of the GSM mobile telephone system.

National Exchange Carrier Association (NECA)

www.neca.org

NECA is a membership association of US local telephone companies. It manages a significant part of the rural telephone industry's revenue streams so people in areas served by small rural telephone companies can stay connected to the rest of America.

National Rural Telecommunications Cooperative (NRTC)

www.nrtc.coop

NRTC represents the advanced telecommunications and information technology interests of 1,500 rural utilities and affiliates in 48 US states. It assists rural electric and telephone utilities in strengthening their businesses with solutions suited to the needs of rural consumers.

National Telecommunications Cooperative Association (NTCA)

www.ntca.org

NTCA is an association of small, rural telecommunications providers which is dedicated to improving the quality of life in rural communities through advanced telecommunications.

Organization for the Promotion and Advancement of Small Telecommunications Companies (OPASTCO)

www.opastco.org

OPASTCO specializes in rural telecom policy, technical issues, member-run committees, education, knowledge-sharing, and networking.

Personal Communications Industry Association (PCIA)

www.pcia.com

PCIA is a trade association representing the companies that make up the wireless telecommunications infrastructure industry.

Telecommunications Industry Association (TIA)

www.tiaonline.org

The Telecommunications Industry Association (TIA) is a trade association representing the global information and communications technology industries.

UMTS Forum

www.umts-forum.org

UMTS Forum is an international association that promotes the global uptake of 3G/UMTS networks.

USTelecom Association

www.ustelecom.org

USTelecom is a trade association representing broadband service providers, manufacturers, and suppliers providing advanced applications and entertainment. USTelecom member companies provide broadband on a fixed and mobile basis, and offer a wide range of voice, data, and video services.

Wi-Fi Alliance

www.wi-fi.org

Wi-Fi Alliance is an organization with the goal of driving adoption and interoperability of wireless local area network products based on IEEE 802.11 specification for Wi-Fi.

WiMAX Forum

www.wimaxforum.org

WiMAX Forum is an organization formed to certify and promote the compatibility and interoperability of broadband wireless products based upon the IEEE 802.16 standard.

Regulation

European Commission

http://ec.europa.eu/information_society/policy/ecomm/index_en.htm

The European Commission created the Communications Committee to assist in carrying out its executive powers under the regulatory framework governing telecoms in the EU.

Federal Communications Commission (FCC)

www.fcc.gov

The FCC was established by the Communications Act of 1934 and is charged with regulating US interstate and international communications by radio, television, wire, satellite, and cable.

Industry Canada

www.ic.gc.ca

Industry Canada's mission is to foster a growing, competitive, knowledge-based Canadian economy. It's also a good source of Telecom regulation.

International Telecommunication Union (ITU)

www.itu.int

ITU is the leading United Nations agency for information and communication on technology issues and is a resource for governments and the private sector in developing networks and services.

National Association of Regulatory Utility Commissioners (NARUC)

www.naruc.org

NARUC represents the State Public Service Commissioners who regulate essential utility services, including energy, telecommunications, and water. NARUC members are responsible for assuring reliable utility service at fair, just, and reasonable rates.

National Telecommunications and Information Administration (NTIA)

www.ntia.doc.gov

NTIA is an agency in the US Department of Commerce that serves as the executive branch agency principally responsible for advising the president on telecommunications and information policies.

Periodicals

Cabling Installation & Maintenance
www.cablinginstall.com
Cabling provides monthly magazine and weekly e-mail newsletters that focus on technical and business information for
structural cabling.

Communications News
www.comnews.com
Communication News is a monthly magazine that sends peri-
odic e-mails regarding networking, voice, data, and video
communications.

FierceTelecom
www.fiercetelecom.com
A daily newsletter focused on next generation networks,
WiMAX, backhaul, and other network and service
innovations.

Inside Telephony
www.insidetelephony.com
Inside Telephony is an information-oriented website that covers wireline, wireless, VoIP, and a slew of other telecom
subjects.

Lightwave
www.lightwaveonline.com
Lightwave is a magazine covering fiber-optic communications
technology and applications for manufacturing, service,
and end-users.

Network World
www.networkworld.com
Network World offers a daily newsletter and various news stories and editorials about networking on its website.

PHONE+
www.phoneplusmag.com
PHONE+ is a monthly trade publication for communication distribution channels; it provides news and strategic
information.

RCR Wireless

www.rcrwireless.com

RCR publishes a portfolio of media and information products enabling intelligence on all things wireless.

Telecom Asia

www.telecomasia.net

Telecom Asia publishes magazines, newsletters, and a website covering regional telecom markets across the globe.

Telecommunications Reports

www.aspenpublishers.com

www.tr.com

Through newsletters, news wires, online services, and special reports, Telecommunications Reports provides information on a wide range of topics, including domestic and international telecom business and policy strategies.

Telephony

www.telephonyonline.com

Telephony is a magazine for communications service providers: new and incumbent, wireline and wireless. It covers news, technologies, and business strategies driving the industry.

TIA's Telecommunications Market Review and Forecast

www.tiaonline.org/business/research/mrf/index.cfm

The *Review and Forecast* is an annual publication that covers a wide range of topics and provides statistics.

Urgent Communications

www.urgentcomm.com

Urgent Communications is a magazine that concentrates on mobile communications, systems, and base stations.

VON/xchange

www.von.com

VON/xchange offers analysis and news for advanced IP communications and traditional telephony.

Warren Communications News

www.warren-news.com

Warren offers a variety of different Telecom newsletters. The *Telecom A.M.* is designed to provide a quick read of significant news each morning. The *Washington Telecom Newswire* provides several e-mails a day with breaking telecom news. The *Communications Daily* is its flagship product and offers daily telecom news. Every two weeks, the *State Telephone Regulation Report* is published; as its names implies, it's focused on state regulation in the US.

Wireless Week

www.wirelessweek.com

Wireless Week provides information on the people, companies, technologies, and ideas that are transforming the wireless industry.

Notes

Chapter 1: Telecom Basics

1. Global Financial Data, Inc. Monthly total return figures 1/31/1962–12/31/2009.
2. Ibid.
3. MSCI. The MSCI information may be used only for your internal use, may not be reproduced or redisseminated in any form and may not be used to create any financial instruments or products or any indices. The MSCI information is provided on an "as is" basis, and the user of this information assumes the entire risk of any use made of this information. MSCI, each of its affiliates, and each other person involved in or related to compiling, computing or creating any MSCI information (collectively, the "MSCI Parties") expressly disclaims all warranties (including, without limitation, any warranties of originality, accuracy, completeness, timeliness, non-infringement, merchantability, and fitness for a particular purpose) with respect to this information. Without limiting any of the foregoing, in no event shall any MSCI Party have any liability for any direct, indirect, special, incidental, punitive, consequential (including, without limitation, lost profits) or any other damages.
4. See note 3.
5. OECD, "OECD Communications Outlook 2009: Executive Summary" (2009), www.oecd.org/dataoecd/24/32/43472431.pdf (accessed November 10, 2010), p. 13.
6. Ibid.
7. Copyright © 2010 The McGraw-Hill Companies, Inc. Standard & Poor's including its subsidiary corporations (S&P) is a division of the McGraw-Hill Companies, Inc. Reproduction of this Work in any form is prohibited without S&P's prior written permission.
8. Hank Intven, *Telecommunications Regulation Handbook*, The World Bank, November 2000, www.infodev.org/en/Publication.22.html, pp. 1–2, (accessed 11/09/2010).

Chapter 2: A Brief History of the Telecom Industry

1. Adjusted for inflation (CPI). Calculated using the US Bureau of Labor Statistics Inflation Calculator. http://data.bls.gov/cgi-bin/cpicalc.pl Note: Calculator only goes back to 1913. An annual inflation of 2.5% was assumed from 1880 to 1913.
2. Adam D. Thierer, "Unnatural Monopoly: Critical Moments in the Development of the Bell System Monopoly," *The Cato Journal* (Fall 1994), www.cato.org/pubs/journal/cjv14n2-6.html (accessed 11/09/2010).

3. Leondard S. Hyman, Richard C. Toole, and Rosemary M. Avellis, *The New Telecommunications Industry: Evolution and Organization* (Public Utility Reports, May 1987).
4. Ibid.
5. Gerald W. Brock, *The Telecommunications Industry: The Dynamics of Market Structure* (Harvard University Press, June 1981).
6. See note 3.
7. See note 5.
8. See note 3.
9. Adjusted for inflation (CPI). Calculated using the US Bureau of Labor Statistics Inflation Calculator. http://data.bls.gov/cgi-bin/cpicalc.pl (accessed 11/09/2010).
10. Ibid.
11. See note 2.
12. *Statistics of Communications Common Carriers*, 2006/2007 Edition, US Federal Communications Commission, www.fcc.gov/Daily_Releases/Daily_Business/2010/db0916/DOC-301505A1.pdf (accessed 11/09/2010).
13. Ibid.

Chapter 3: Telecom Sector Composition

1. "6.1.2 Per Capita and Household Expenditure on Communications," ICT Regulation Toolkit, www.ictregulationtoolkit.org/en/Section.3337.html (accessed 11/09/2010).
2. Thomson Reuters, MSCI ACWI Index, as of 12/31/09.
3. See Chapter 1, note 3.
4. See note 2.
5. Ibid.
6. See Chapter 1, note 3.

Chapter 4: Telecom Sector Drivers

1. See Chapter 1, note 3.

Chapter 5: Consumer Demand

1. Andre Levisse, Nimal Manuel, and Martin Sjolund, "Getting More From Prepaid Mobile Services," *McKinsey Quarterly* (February 2008), www.mckinseyquarterly.com/Getting_more_from_prepaid_mobile_services_2108 (accessed November 10, 2010).
2. Ericsson, "Pre-paid Subscribers in Charge," (March 19, 2010), www.ericsson.com/news/1395590 (accessed November 10, 2010).
3. IDC, "Worldwide Smartphone Market Grows 89.5% Year Over Year in Third Quarter as New Devices Launch, Says IDC" (November 4, 2010), www.idc.com/about/viewpressrelease.jsp?containerId=prUS22560610&sectionId=null&elementId=null&pageType=SYNOPSIS (accessed November 10, 2010).
4. AT&T, "AT&T Leads the US in Smartphones and Integrated Devices" (May 15, 2009), www.att.com/gen/press-room?pid=4800&cdvn=news&newsarticleid=26819 (accessed November 10, 2010).

5. Organisation for Economic Co-operation and Development, "OECD Communications Outlook 2009: Executive Summary" (2009), www.oecd.org/dataoecd/24/32/43472431 .pdf (accessed November 10, 2010), p. 15.
6. Ibid.

Chapter 6: Challenges and Opportunities

1. Verizon, "Fiber to the Premises (FTTP)," www22.verizon.com/about/community/tx/ technology/technology.html (accessed November 11, 2010).
2. Amy Standen, "The Phone Book's Days Appear Numbered" (January 18, 2010), NPR, www.npr.org/templates/story/story.php?storyId=122693536 (accessed November 11, 2010).
3. Ibid.
4. Ibid.

Chapter 7: The Top-Down Method

1. Matthew Kalman, "Einstein Letters Reveal a Turmoil Beyond Science," *Boston Globe* (July 11, 2006), www.boston.com/news/world/middleeast/articles/2006/07/11/ einstein_letters_reveal_a_turmoil_beyond_science/ (accessed December 10, 2009).
2. Michael Michalko, "Combinatory Play," Creative Thinking, www.creativethinking. net/DT10_CombinatoryPlay.htm?Entry=Good (accessed December 10, 2009).
3. Gary P. Brinson, Brian D. Singer, and Gilbert L. Beebower, "Determinants of Portfolio Performance II: An Update," *Financial Analysts Journal* 47 (1991), 3.
4. See Chapter 1, note 3.
5. Ibid.
6. Ibid.
7. Ibid.
8. Ibid.
9. Ibid.

Glossary

Access charge   A monthly fee imposed by the Federal Communications Commission on all phone customers (except Lifeline customers) for access to the long distance network. It's also called a network access charge.

Analog   A transmission method using continuous electrical signals that vary in amplitude or frequency in response to changes in sound, light, pressure, or position.

Average revenue per user (ARPU)   A measure of revenue on a per user or subscriber basis (revenue divided by the number of subscribers). ARPU allows companies to track revenue sources and growth.

Backbone   The large transmission line that carries data gathered from small lines that interconnect with it.

Bandwidth   The smallest range of frequencies that can be transmitted without distortion. It's measured as the number of bits that can be transferred per second. Greater bandwidths have a higher information carrying capacity.

Bell System   A term for AT&T prior to its 1984 divestiture, which included 24 Bell operating companies providing local exchange phone service, the AT&T Long Lines Division providing long distance connections, equipment manufacturing (Western Electric), and a research and development arm (Bell Laboratories).

Bit   The smallest unit of digital information utilized by electronic or optical information processing, storage, or transmission systems. Bit is short for binary digit. Binary technology is based on the representation of data with 0s and 1s, whose combinations form a protocol medium for all data transmission.

Bundles   A marketing strategy that involves offering several different products for sale as one combined product. The rate structure provides a financial or other benefit that is usually contingent on the use, consumption, or subscription to all the service elements in the bundle.

Byte   A byte consists of eight bits and represents the amount of data of a number or letter. It's also the smallest unit of information that a computer system can locate within its data storage or memory.

Carrier   A telecom provider that owns circuit-switching equipment. In contrast, resellers provide phone services but don't own the switching equipment. Also called a service provider.

CDMA (code division multiple access)   A spread spectrum air interface protocol that uses radio frequencies to provide mobile telecom services, including interoperability with the wireline PSTN (public switched telephone network). CDMA was developed by Qualcomm and is one of three main protocol implementations used in delivering mobile voice services.

Churn rate   A measure of customer turnover. It's used especially in the mobile telephony or Internet access markets and is usually measured as a rate per month. The calculation is the number of subscribers that terminated service divided by the average number of customers in the network during the period.

Circuit switching   A switching system in which a dedicated physical circuit path exists between a sender and receiver for the duration of the call.

CLEC (competitive local exchange carrier)   A company that provides local wireline phone service and competes with an incumbent local exchange carrier (ILEC). CLECs were formed in response to the Telecom Act of 1996, which aimed to increase local carrier competition.

Coaxial cable (coax) A copper wire surrounded by insulation which is itself surrounded by a grounded shield of braided wire. The coax minimizes electrical and radio frequency interference. Coaxial cable is the most common type of cabling used for network access lines that deliver television and other audio-visual signals into customer premises.

Common carrier A company offering telecommunications services or facilities to the public.

Cramming Adding services and charges for enhanced features such as voicemail, caller ID, and call-waiting that customers have not ordered.

Data compression Techniques (usually mathematic algorithms) to reduce data's size so less disk space storage and transmission time is required to manage it.

Default carrier A customer's direct dial carrier. By calling 1-700-555-4141, a caller can identify his default carrier.

Digital Subscriber Line (DSL) A generic name for a group of enhanced speed digital services provided by telephone service providers. DSL services run on twisted-pair wires; they carry both voice and data.

Ethernet A networking protocol developed by Xerox Corp. that is used in local area networks (LANs).

Exchange A unit generally smaller than a LATA, established by the local exchange carrier (LEC) for the administration of communications service in a specified area (usually a city, town, or village and its environs). An exchange consists of one or more central offices together with the associated facilities used to provide communications services within that area. Multiple exchanges make up a LATA.

Facilities Transmission lines, switches, and other physical components used to provide telephone service.

Federal Communications Commission (FCC) An independent agency of the US government, which was established by the Communications Act of 1934 to regulate the Telecom sector. It oversees licenses, rates, tariffs, standards, limitations, and so on.

Federal Subscriber Line Charge Also know as a Federal Access Charge, Customer Line Charge, Interstate Access Charge, Interstate Single Line Charge, FCC Approved Customer Line Charge, Subscriber Line Charge, or SLC. It's a federally mandated charge billed by local telephone companies and pays part of the cost of supplying a phone line to a home or business to the local telephone company. It is designed to help local phone companies recover the cost of providing "local loops." It's not a tax, but a charge that is part of the price you pay to your local telephone company. Neither the FCC nor any other government agency receives the Federal Subscriber Line Charge, and the FCC places a cap on the charge.

Fiber optics Technology based on transferring information over thin filaments of glass or other transparent materials. Coded light pulses that represent data, image, and sound are transmitted at higher speeds than more conventional materials, like copper.

GSM (global system for mobile) GSM is the most popular standard for mobile telephony systems in the world. GSM differs from its predecessor technologies in that both signaling and speech channels are digital, and thus GSM is considered a second generation (2G) mobile phone system.

High definition television (HDTV) An improved television system which provides video with approximately twice the vertical and horizontal resolution of pre-existing television standards. It also provides audio quality approaching that of compact discs.

Incumbent Local Exchange Carrier (ILEC) An ILEC provides telephone exchange services in a specific region. The regional boundaries for ILECs were determined by the Telecommunications Act of 1996.

Intercarrier payment   Expenses payable to another telecommunications service provider for a range of services, such as the transmission and termination of traffic, roaming charges, and services either for administrative purposes or to provide telecommunications services or facilities.

Interexchange carrier   A long distance company providing long-distance phone service between LATAs. Also called IEC and IXC.

Internet Service Provider (ISP)   Any service provider, including providers of voice telephony or cable television services that provides Internet connectivity or an Internet-based application on a retail or wholesale basis. ISPs may provide additional services, such as e-mail accounts and remote data file storage.

ISDN (Integrated Services Digital Network)   ISDN integrates speech and data on the same lines by providing access to packet switched networks over ordinary telephone copper wires. Prior to ISDN, phone lines were used overwhelmingly for voice, with limited data services.

LAN (local area network)   LAN is a transmission network encompassing a limited area, such as a single building or several buildings in close proximity. In such a small geographic area, leased telecommunication lines are not needed to link computers and devices.

Landline   Traditional wired phone service.

LATA (local access transport area)   A geographic service area established in accordance with the Modification of Final Judgment (MFJ) in order to define the area within which a telephone company may offer services.

LEC (local exchange carrier)   The local or regional telephone company that owns and operates lines to customer locations. It can be either an independent company or a Bell Operating Company.

Local loop   The communications channel, usually a physical line, between the customer's premises and the edge of the telecom service provider's network. It's also known as a subscriber loop.

MMS (multimedia messaging service)   A wireless messaging service that adds images, text, audio clips, and video clips to SMS (Short Message Service/text messaging).

Mobile data   Mobile data is wireless data transmission to a hand-held device, such as a smartphone or PDA. Mobile data plans have provided a growing source of revenue for telecom firms due to the popularity of smartphones.

Mobile penetration rate   Measures the number of mobile subscribers per 100 inhabitants and is usually represented as a percentage figure.

Modification of Final Judgment (MFJ)   The 1982 US federal court judgment that set the rules and regulations concerning deregulation and divestiture of AT&T and the Bell system.

Multiplexing   An electronic or optical process that combines a large number of lower-speed transmission lines into one high-speed line by splitting the total available bandwidth of the high-speed line into narrower bands (frequency division). The same result can be achieved by allotting a common channel to several different transmitting devices, one at a time in sequence (time division). Multiplexing devices are widely employed in networks to improve efficiency by concentrating traffic.

Network   Any system designed to provide one or more access paths for communications between users at different geographic locations. Networks may utilize circuit or message switching that route messages based on unique addresses for recipients.

OEM (original equipment manufacturer)   The manufacturer of products that are resold by another vendor who usually substitutes its name on the product for that of the manufacturer.

Packet   A group of binary digits switched over a digital network. When data has to be transmitted, it is broken down into similar structures of data, which are reassembled in the original data chunk when they reach their destination.

Packet switched network   A digital data transmission network that uses packet switching technology.

Packet switching   A digital data transmission method that divides messages and files into standard-size pieces (packets) that are switched across networks individually and then reassembled at their destination.

Prepaid calling card   A card or virtual card that is bought in advance entitling the owner to make phone calls. When the owner of the card makes phone calls, the value of the card decreases at a predetermined rate per minute.

Public Utilities Commission (PUC)   The agency regulating intrastate phone service.

RBOCs (regional Bell operating companies)   RBOCs resulted from the 1982 AT&T antitrust settlement with the US Department of Justice, in which it agreed to divest its local service companies. The seven resulting independent RBOCs are also known as the "Baby Bells."

Reseller   A company that does not own transmission facilities. It purchases telecommunications services at wholesale and sells them to the public for profit. Also known as a Resale Carrier.

Roaming   A tariff charged by mobile communications network operators which allows a subscriber to use a cell phone outside of the local calling area. The tariff is usually measured by minute, data, or message. There are often at least two charges: an end-user retail charge paid by the end-user to a service provider, and an intercarrier retail charge paid from one service provider to another for network use.

Router   An electronic device that intercepts signals on a computer network. The router determines where the signals have to go. Each signal it receives is called a data packet, and the packet contains address information that the router uses to divert signals appropriately.

Satellite   A satellite communications system is composed of earth stations that communicate with each other via a radio relay station that orbits the earth—a satellite. Satellites are used to transmit a variety of data signals, including telephone and television.

Service area   An area within which a local phone company provides services. Also called a local access transport area (LATA).

Service plan   The rate plan you select when beginning wireless phone service. A service plan typically consists of a monthly base rate for access to the system and a fixed amount of minutes per month. Various service plans are offered to be cost-effective for different types of customers. Also called a rate plan.

Service provider   A telecom provider that owns circuit-switching equipment. In contrast, resellers provide phone services but don't own the switching equipment. Also called a carrier.

SMS (short messaging service)   A wireless messaging service that permits the transmission of a short text message from and to a digital mobile telephone, regardless of whether the transmission originates and terminates on a mobile telephone. SMS messages can be up to 160 characters.

Spectrum   The range of electromagnetic radio frequencies used in the transmission of data, sound, and television.

Subscriber Line Charge (SLC)   A monthly fee paid by telephone subscribers that is used to compensate the local telephone company for part of the cost of installation and maintenance of the telephone wire, poles, and other facilities that link your home to the telephone network, aka the local loop.

Switch A device that can be controlled to interconnect two circuits.

Telecommunications As defined in the Telecommunications Act of 1996: the transmission between or among points specified by the user, of information of the user's choosing, without change in the form or content of the information as sent and received. Any transmission, emission, or reception of signs, signals, writings, images, and sounds or intelligence by wire, radio, optical, or other electromagnetic systems.

Telephony The technology of transmitting voice over distances via a telecommunications network.

Twisted pair A cable consisting of two solid copper strands twisted around each other. The twisting provides a measure of protection from electromagnetic and radio-frequency interference.

Unbundling Local exchange carriers providing other service providers access to buy or lease portions of their networks to serve subscribers.

Universal Service Fund Fee (USF) Also known as Universal Service Fund Charge or Universal Service Charge. This charge started on January 1, 1998, as part of the FCC overhaul of telephone fees. The USF fee is a charge collected by telecommunications carriers for federal and state funds that support the provision of affordable communications services to rural, isolated, and high-cost regions of the country; low-income residential consumers; schools, libraries, and rural health care. Telecom companies are required by law to contribute to this fund, but the law does not prohibit companies from passing this charge on to customers.

VoIP (voice over internet protocol) Any of a family of methodologies, communication protocols, and transmission technologies for delivery of voice communications and multimedia over Internet Protocol (IP) networks, such as the Internet.

WAN (wide area network) A computer network that extends over a broad area. It usually connects LANs to other LANs using communications lines provided by a common carrier.

Wavelength The distance between a point on one lightwave and the point of corresponding phase on the following lightwave. Lightwaves can be divided into wavelength portions and deployed as a series of communications channels. Although the bandwidth supplied by these channels is a function of the equipment deployed at their ends, most commercial wavelength products are offered in standard bandwidth increments, especially 2.5 Gbps and 10 Gbps.

Wi-Fi (802.11) A limited-range wireless networking protocol based on the 802.11 family of standards, which enables a device such as a personal computer, video game console, smartphone, or digital audio player to connect to the Internet.

About the Authors

Dan Sinton is a Research Analyst at Fisher Investments. Prior to joining Fisher, he worked at Franklin Templeton, Charles Schwab, and in the nonprofit sector. Dan received a BA in International Affairs at the University of Colorado and an MBA from Georgetown University. He currently lives in San Francisco, California.

Andrew S. Teufel has been with Fisher Investments since 1995, where he currently serves as Vice Chairman. Prior to joining Fisher Investments, he worked at Bear Stearns as a corporate finance analyst in its Global Technology Group. Andrew also instructs at many seminars and educational workshops throughout the US and UK and has lectured at the Haas School of Business at UC Berkeley. He is also the Editor in Chief of MarketMinder.com. Andrew is a graduate of UC Berkeley.

Index

Printed and bound by CPI Group (UK) Ltd, Croydon, CR0 4YY

16/04/2025

14658510-0005